Bill O'Reilly

D0375629

A
BOLD
Fresh Piece
of
HUMANITY

Broadway Books

New York

BROADWAY BOOKS and the Broadway Books colophon
are trademarks of Random House, Inc.

Originally published in hardcover in the United States by
Broadway Books, New York, in 2008.

Lyrics to the St. Brigid's School song were adapted from "Open Up Your
Heart (And Let the Sunshine In)" by Stuart Hamblen.

Movie poster on page 46 and movie still on page 48 courtesy of
Photofest. Group photo on page 173 courtesy of Visko Hatfield.
All other photos from the author's collection.

Library of Congress Cataloging-in-Publication Data
O'Reilly, Bill.
A bold fresh piece of humanity: a —memoir/by Bill O'Reilly.
p.   cm.
1. O'Reilly, Bill.   2. Journalists—United
States—Biography.   I. Title.

PN4874.O73A3 2008
070.92—dc22
[B]   2008025510

ISBN 978-0-7679-2883-0

Printed in the United States of America

Book design by Michael Collica

1 3 5 7 9 10 8 6 4 2

First Paperback Edition

This book is dedicated to all Factor
viewers, listeners, and readers.

You guys keep me going.

State of grace? You make the call.

Don't look back,
You can never look back.

        —Don Henley, "The Boys of Summer"

CONTENTS

x

Contents

A
BOLD
Fresh Piece
of
HUMANITY

Reading This Book Will Dramatically Improve Your Life!

G ot your attention, didn't I? Hopefully, that hyped-up statement will prove to be true, although I fully realize there will be skeptics. After all, I've had four consecutive number one nonfiction best sellers, so what is there left to say? I mean, come on, everybody knows O'Reilly is a champion bloviator, but is another book *really* necessary?

I think so.

You see, I've never really explained how I got to be that showy bloviator; I have not defined exactly how my opinions, which so rankle more than a few sensitive souls, were formed. So that's what this book is all about: defining the experiences that have shaped my thinking, propelling me into becoming one of the most controversial human beings in the world. Also, I think you'll find the following pages interesting on a number of other levels besides my life experience. This book is full of stories and references that, perhaps, were important in your life as well. By design, much of the story is about me but not *all* about me. Thank God.

We can't begin at the real beginning, September 10, 1949, because not much was happening in my world at that time. I was just a normal baby, nothing unusual. No strange-looking eyes like those *Village of the Damned* kids.

Wow, were they spooky or what? To this day, I remember those urchins scaring the Milk Duds out of me in a dark Long Island movie theater.

No, my point of view really began taking shape at age four, when, in a New York neighborhood teeming with children, playtime became an intense experience. A few years later, my intellectual development (such as it was) started to accelerate at a Catholic grammar

My third-grade class. That's the bold, fresh
guy on Sister Lurana's right.

school that was simply unforgettable. And it is at that school where this story begins.

The year was 1957, the month September, and I had just turned eight years old. Dwight Eisenhower was President, but in my life it was the diminutive, intense Sister Mary Lurana who ruled, at least in the third-grade class where I was held captive. For reasons you will soon understand, my parents had remanded me to the penal institution of St. Brigid's School in Westbury, New York, a cruel and unusual punishment if there ever was one.

Already, I had barely survived my first two years at St. Brigid's because I was, well, a little nitwit. Not satisfied with memorizing *The Baltimore Catechism*'s fine prose, which featured passages like, "God made me to show His goodness and to make me happy with Him in heaven," I was constantly annoying my classmates and, of course, the no-nonsense Sister Lurana. With sixty overactive students in her class, she was understandably short on patience. For survival, she had also become quick on the draw.

Then it happened. One day I blurted out some dumb remark and Sister Lurana was on me like a panther. Her black habit blocked out all distractions as she leaned down, looked me in the eye, and uttered words I have never forgotten: "William, you are a bold, fresh piece of humanity."

And she was dead-on.

The following pages will prove that the sister's perspicacious remark remains relevant about fifty years after the fact. But this account is not a traditional memoir in the sense that I mean to tell you my life story. I don't want to do that, because I happen to think I'm a pretty boring guy. So a recitation of my existence wouldn't do anyone much good. Instead, I will attempt to define *why* I believe *what* I believe by telling you how those convictions grew directly out of my life experience. This tactic is designed to keep you, the reader, entertained and amused, as you and I probably have much in common, at least in the upbringing department.

Once out of childhood, the adult bold, fresh piece of humanity got around, visiting more than seventy countries, observing four wars up close and personal, meeting thousands of people, and having millions of laughs. So we'll take a look at some of that stuff in relation to important issues like war, peace, prosperity, and your daily

The O'Reilly family in our
Levittown backyard.

life. Since millions of you listen to my bloviations on TV and radio, this book might provide some clarity, bonding (hate that word), and even some sympathy (although I don't seek it).

Also, the following pages just might tee some people off even further. Either way, we'll have some fun.

If you know my work, you might have figured out that I am not a philosopher or a dreamer. I do not live in a theoretical world or gain insights by attempting to read the thoughts of others. Instead, in line with the exhortations of Teddy Roosevelt, I embrace a strenuous life. My attitudes about life, liberty, and the pursuit of happiness have been formed by a multitude of unique occurrences that happened directly to me. Some of those events I will share with you, hoping that the sheer ego of the exercise will evaporate as you begin to understand how a doltish, working-class kid from Levittown, Long Island, New York, has "evolved" into perhaps the most controversial journalist and commentator in the United States of America.

I believe Sister Mary Lurana (who, by the way, is still alive and once sent me a very kind letter) is proud of me. Although, in truth, the anguish I put her through cannot ever be fully exorcised, even by a William Peter Blatty character. But there is no doubt that the way I think today has its roots in my traditional childhood home and in the strict Catholic schools I attended. Therefore, we'll take an incisive look at those influences as well as other significant events in the life of O'Reilly, all with an eye toward convincing you that the point of view I bring to the world is worthy, and might even help you in your life.

For starters, it really did all begin in the mid-1950s, when America's population was half of what it is today. Hope as well as the challenge of swift change was in the air. The USA had survived the Great Depression, World War II, and the Korean War. Despite saber rattling by the Soviet Union, things were looking up and everyday life was fairly simple, at least compared to today. You worked, obeyed the law, cared for your family, looked out for your neighbors, and respected your country. At least, that was the creed of the huge working class, which did most of the country's heavy lifting.

That was the background of my family. My father, William O'Reilly Sr., held a decent job, bought a small house, and sired two kids. My mother, Ann O'Reilly, was an energetic stay-at-home mom because, had she not been, one of her kids would be in the penitentiary right now.

Yes, that would be me. My younger sister, Janet, has always been a solid citizen, not at all fresh or bold. The nuns loved her.

So that's the jumping-off point for this book, the white ethnic, basically blue-collar suburbs of America in a conventional time when baby boomers were popping out all over the place. The journey begins at the dinner table, where chewy meat loaf and fish sticks reigned, and in a neighborhood full of kids playing in the streets because our yards were too small.

Oh, and one more thing: Hey, Sister, I can't thank you enough for the title.

CHAPTER

POLITICS

*When they call the roll in the Senate, the Senators do
not know whether to answer "present" or "not guilty."*
—THEODORE ROOSEVELT

I f you watch the bold, fresh guy on television or listen to me on the
radio, you know I'm not a rabidly partisan political guy. I don't
endorse candidates for office or shill for them in any way. Party af-
filiation does not matter to me. Over the years, my philosophy has
evolved into this: I vote for the person who I believe will do the least
amount of damage to the country. It is rare that a true problem solver
is nominated for office, so usually it's who will do the *least* amount
of harm to the folks.

I know that sounds cynical, but let's be honest: politics in America is a money play full of charlatans and crazed ideologues. Once
in a while a person of true principle emerges, but the media usually
quickly destroys that candidate because honesty always, and I mean
always, collides with ideology. Only independent thinkers can de-
liver unbiased appraisals of complicated problems, and indepen-

dent thinkers have little chance to succeed in our two-party system, which demands rigid adherence to left or right doctrine.

My philosophy about what's best for America is spelled out in vivid detail in my last book, *Culture Warrior,* so there's no need to state it again. However, no matter what I say or write, fanatics will attack it because Kool-Aid–drinking ideologues on both sides resent my national platform and nonaligned analysis. I'm amused that the far left attempts to demonize me as a rigid conservative, while at the same time the far right despises me because I'm not reactionary enough. As I always say, as long as the extremists hate me, I know I'm doing my job. So bring it on, Sean Penn and Michael Savage. You guys are totally nuts; it's a compliment that both of you attack me.

The political angst that I now proudly cause began rather early in my life. Thinking back, I realize my first brush with politics happened in 1956, when I heard my mother sing:

I like Ike.
I'll say it again and again.
I like Ike.
Let him finish the job he began.

Since I was just six years old, I didn't "like Ike" because I didn't know who the heck he was. I did know Buffalo Bob and Mighty Mouse, Davy Crockett and Elvis, but not this guy Ike. Both of my parents were traditional people in most ways but were also politically independent. Because the O'Reilly clan comprised mainly civil servants working in New York City, they were loyal Democrats. On my mother's side, the Kennedys and Drakes usually voted Democratic as well.

But the Democrat running against President Eisenhower, Adlai Stevenson, was an avowed social liberal and held zero appeal for my parents, who believed strongly in self-reliance and Judeo-Christian values. Stevenson would say that year, "Trust the people. Trust their good sense." Well, old Adlai shouldn't have been shocked that my folks and most others living in Levittown didn't trust him. Overwhelmingly, they voted for Ike.

One of the reasons was his service. My father was a naval officer during World War II and respected Dwight Eisenhower's perfor-

My father in Japan just after the end of World War II.

mance in the European theater. Back then and still today, traditional people supported the military. Ike won a second term in a landslide.

To me, a fresh but also shallow little kid, politics was really boring. Outside of the St. Brigid's classroom, my childhood was largely one big game. I played four sports: football, baseball, basketball, and ice hockey. When games weren't scheduled, we played stick-ball in the street: cheap game, all you needed was a rubber ball and a broomstick. We also played keep-away and ringolevio (don't ask). We were sweating all the time and had zero interest in public policy. For us, the Cold War took place on a hockey pond in mid-January.

Forced into the Arena

Then in 1960 John F. Kennedy ran for president against Vice President Richard Nixon. Suddenly, there was a split in my house. My mother, a Kennedy on her mom's side, was a JFK supporter. My father went with Nixon, even though he didn't like the man all that much. I don't remember exactly why my parents supported their respective can-didates, but I do recall sitting at the supper table (we never called it dinner) and hearing them tease each other. My mother said they were going to "cancel each other out." I didn't know what that meant and didn't really care. My mom's cooking was so awful I just wanted to get away from the table as fast as possible.

As the election approached, my sixth-grade teacher, a kindly old woman named Mrs. Boyle, came up with an idea. The class should have a debate. And since I never shut up, I was chosen to be one of the debaters. This was not good. I had no idea what a debate was, much less whom I should support. Giants versus Yankees, I knew. Kennedy against Nixon? Total blank.

"So, William," Mrs. Boyle said, "which candidate will you support?"

"Is Davy Crockett running?"

Yes, I actually said that stupid thing. But Mrs. Boyle was used to my nonsense, and so was the class, which considered me a hopeless buffoon. Since I had only two choices, I took Nixon, because my fa-ther was louder than my mother. It's true that was my sole rationale;

Republicans and Democrats didn't even enter into my thinking. Because my dad bloviated more about stuff than my mom, I figured he'd be happy to give me some debating tips.

Forget it.

My father, all six feet four inches, two hundred and ten pounds of him, lumbered home from work every day around six thirty p.m., exactly twelve hours from the time he left for the office in the morning. His job as a money changer for an oil company was boring, and, as stated, my mother's culinary skills were, well, incredibly bad. So, in addition to being exhausted by dull and tedious work, my father was usually hungry. This is not a good combination for a big Irish guy with a temper.

Typically, my sister and I usually avoided Dad until about noon on Saturday. He cooked breakfast on the weekends, which put him in a better frame of mind. My father's cooking was far superior to my mom's and she knew it. But she didn't actually care.

I'm telling you all this because my plan was to have my father write down what I should say about Richard Nixon, to tell me why the guy was the greatest. In that way, I could memorize my father's point of view and dazzle Mrs. Boyle and the class with the wisdom of my dad, which, of course, I would claim as my own. I mean, how great was this strategy?

So, on the eve of the big debate, with pen and paper in hand, I asked my father why he was voting for Nixon. Sitting on the floor, I was poised to write down every single word.

"Because Kennedy's father is a crook," my dad said.

"Really, a crook?" I asked.

"Yep."

"In what way?"

"Sold booze during Prohibition."

Oh. I didn't know what Prohibition actually was, but it sounded good, so I wrote it down, badly misspelling the P-word.

Still, I needed more or it would be a short debate, so I pressed on.

"What about Nixon; why do you like him?"

"Don't like him," my father answered.

"YOU DON'T LIKE HIM?" Almost immediately, I was panicking.

"They're all phonies," my father answered, and went back to watching *The Ed Sullivan Show.*

I remember scribbling in my notebook: *Kennedy's dad is a crook . . . sold booze . . . pro something . . . my dad hates Nixon. They're all phonies.* A vague sense of doom gripped me, but what could I do? My father had spoken and was not a man you badgered for anything.

The next day, Monday, Mrs. Boyle announced that the debate would be held after the lunch recess. On my side were two other young Republicans; on the other side were three Democrats. All I remember about the ensuing fiasco is that I said something about Nixon being tough on the Russians and Kennedy's father being a crook. The other side totally ignored me and hammered home just one emphatic point: JOHN FITZGERALD KENNEDY WAS CATHOLIC!

They won the debate by a landslide.

Fine with me. That debating business was far too much work. Back then, if anyone had ever suggested that I would eventually become famous for debating on television, Mrs. Boyle would have called the mental health authorities to take a close look at the child who had suggested it.

After the election, the new Kennedy administration impacted me only because of the fallout-shelter drills at school. Once in a while a bell rang and all the St. Brigid's kids had to file out to the school parking lot, where, we were told, if a random atom bomb happened to fall nearby, buses would whisk us away to some underground bunker. Nobody seemed very concerned about it, but a few years later, the Cuban missile crisis did get the attention of the smarter kids.

But, obviously, I was not one of the smarter kids. *American Bandstand* had more influence on me than President Kennedy or any other politician. In fact, about the only time I locked in on Kennedy was when comedian Vaughn Meader did a dead-on impression of him on TV. There was also a song called "My Daddy Is President" by a kid trying to imitate Caroline Kennedy, the President's young daughter. I remember thinking the song was stupid, which is somewhat incomprehensible, since I liked a Christmas song recorded by singers imitating chipmunks. It was that kind of taste and logic that defined me as a child.

The End of Innocence

The political thing became more focused for me on November 22, 1963, when the loudspeaker in Brother Carmine Diodati's religion class crackled and on came a radio report of President Kennedy's assassination in Dallas. By then, I was a freshman at Chaminade High School and this was big Kennedy territory. The following days featured a number of sorrowful Masses and lectures about the slain President and the tragedy that had befallen America.

At home, my parents never said much about the murder itself but were glued to Walter Cronkite for information. I remember that my father didn't much care for Lyndon Johnson, who was distant to him in many ways. My mother was mostly worried about Jackie Kennedy and her two young children.

But, all in all, politics and the issues of the day did not intrude very much on the O'Reilly family situation. We soldiered on, so to speak, without much partisan activity. It was the same thing on the street; I can never remember my friends discussing politics at all. Why would you? We had the Yankees, Mets, Giants, Jets, Rangers, and Knicks. It was exhausting.

Then came the summer of 1967, the Summer of Love in San Francisco. For us teenagers in my Levittown neighborhood, love was often demonstrated in cars on dark lanes. But as Bob Dylan sang, the times were a-changin'. Vietnam began heating up, and a few of the older guys came home injured from Southeast Asia. Some others showed up with completely altered personalities. For the first time in my life, I saw close up what war could do. Curious, I talked with some of the returning vets, and they all said the same thing: Vietnam was chaos; there was nothing good about it.

That fall, I entered Marist College in Poughkeepsie, New York, exempt from the draft on a student deferment. Most of the neighborhood guys who did not have that advantage were called up, and many shipped out to Southeast Asia. One neighborhood guy came home from Vietnam and killed himself. Another became a hard-core drug addict. Like everyone else, I saw the fighting on television and heard the intense debates. So I decided to ask my father about it. He said the war was a disaster, nothing like World War II, when the country was united against enemies that had directly attacked us. He didn't further explain his opinion, but his blunt words overrode everything else on the subject, as far as I was concerned. My father was a tough guy, sometimes irrational in his anger over petty stuff. But he never lied to me and he was not uninformed. If he thought the Vietnam situation was screwed up, it was screwed up.

As opposition to the war mounted throughout the country, I paid more attention, but typically, I was essentially detached from most of it. Playing football for Marist College, socializing, and occasionally studying occupied most of my time. Even though not pro-war, my father and many other Levittowners were rapidly becoming appalled by the often outlandish behavior displayed by hard-core antiwar activists. Abbie Hoffman, Jerry Rubin, and the rest of the militant protesters brought a few choice words from LTJG William O'Reilly Sr. As a former naval officer, he didn't like drugs, he didn't like sloppy appearances, and he didn't like the pounding music from Iron Butterfly. He wasn't overly angry with the yippies and hippies; he was more confused by them. What had happened to America?

I rarely discussed the state of the country with my father during my summers at home, because we were both working long hours. He was still a low-level bean counter, and I made money as a swimming instructor for the Town of Babylon on Long Island. One night, however, I did play him a cut from the new Doors album. I can't remember why I did such an inexplicable thing, but I do clearly recall his terse response: "Stick with Elvis."

Okay.

At the same time, my father recoiled from the "America right or wrong" crowd. He wanted effective leadership in Washington, not fatuous propaganda. As the war foundered, his opinion of President Johnson and the Democratic establishment cratered, and, without viable options in the campaign of 1968, my father was forced again to support Richard Nixon for President. As they say in *MAD* magazine: yeeesh.

Meanwhile, my college career was going the way that most college careers go: I did my work, tried and failed to beguile young ladies, and had a load of mindless fun without getting loaded. Well, I might be a bit unusual in that last category. You'll get a more thorough explanation later.

Also, because I had begun writing for the college newspaper, I started paying closer attention to world events, which were growing more chaotic by the week, both at home and abroad. Still, at Marist College, the antiwar movement was rather placid, because most of the students there were sons and daughters of working people: cops, firemen, salesmen, and the like. Those folks were not real enthusiastic about chanting, "Hey, hey, LBJ, how many kids did you kill today?" Trust me, few were burning flags and/or bras in Levittown.

Till It's Over—Over There

In the spring of 1969, a life-altering thing happened. Some of my college friends were accepted to the Third Year Abroad program and suggested I apply as well. I didn't jump at the prospect right away. Because I was playing football, writing for the paper, and had figured out how to get relatively good grades for the least amount of work, I was not all that intrigued with the prospect of going to a foreign country, where I might actually have to bust my butt academically and give up football. But, finally, I decided to apply.

I was turned down!

Outrage gripped me. Turned down? Are you kidding me? My grades were better than most of those accepted, and I even spent more than an hour writing the damn Third Year Abroad essay explaining my desire to "accelerate my knowledge." It was complete BS, but so were all the other essays. What the heck was going on?

The answer to that question takes us back to my experience in grammar school: remember when I was labeled a "bold, fresh piece of humanity"? The problem, according to some Marist teachers, was that I was still simply that. In the eyes of my instructors, I had not evolved very much from the little wise guy that Sister Lurana had accurately branded. In short, I was a Philistine who could not be trusted to represent the college in a sophisticated foreign country—or any other destination, for that matter.

Oh, yeah?

Now, I'm the type of guy who does not readily accept the word *no*. I've succeeded in my career because the more negative things said about me, the harder I work to disprove them. Living well is not the best revenge. Succeeding in your career and humiliating your critics is.

Anyway, I demanded that the professors running the abroad program explain themselves or I would write an article accusing them of anti-Irish bias. Or anti-Levittown bias. Or whatever bias I could conjure up. In a tense meeting, I explained to those pinheads that I studied hard, had achieved a high grade point average, had avoided any misdemeanor or felony convictions, and actually attended church most every Sunday.

On my way to England in 1969.

So what say you, Professors?

They folded. I was accepted into the program. The problem was, I didn't actually *want* to go abroad. But I had caused such a ruckus that, in September 1969, I found myself on an ocean liner sailing from New York City to Southampton, England. Accompanying me were hundreds of other students, many of whom were long-haired, pot-fueled male maniacs who did far better with the female passengers than I did.

Plus, I got seasick. Not good at all.

When I arrived in London to begin my courses at Queen Mary College, a satellite of the University of London, I immediately ran into a lot of anti-American feeling. The Vietnam War, of course, was just as unpopular in Great Britain as it was in the USA, but there was also an undercurrent of hostility toward the American system in general. In my student dormitory, Commonwealth Hall, some of the "blokes" actually disliked me solely because of my citizenship!

Certainly we all can understand loathing me because of personality issues, but embracing hate simply because I was born in the USA? Completely unacceptable.

One guy named Derek consistently gave me a hard time about my New Yawk accent. It was clear to him that everything in British culture was far superior to anything America had to offer. I found this kind of amusing, since the highest-rated TV program in England in 1969 was *Top of the Pops,* a rip-off of *American Bandstand.* And, for much of the year, the highest-rated song on that program was a ditty by a group called Edison Lighthouse that featured this perceptive chorus:

Love grows where my Rosemary goes,
and nobody knows like me.

As the British are fond of saying: indeed.

Anyway, I annoyed Derek by mocking the *Pops,* and he continued on about my speech patterns until I let loose with this bit of intellectual wisdom: "Hey, bud, you'd have a *German* accent if it wasn't for my father and thousands of other New Yorkers like him. So *blank* you, fish and chips, and the Beatles. Get me?"

Make friends everywhere; that's always been my motto. Somewhere in Poughkeepsie, the head of the abroad program was weeping.

The anti-Americanism I witnessed in the dorm, during antiwar demonstrations in Trafalgar Square, in the British classrooms, and on the BBC, did not go down real well with me. I was no fan of the Vietnam War, but even at nineteen years old, I loved my country and understood its essential nobility. America is not a perfect place, but the good heavily outweighs the bad, and those who despise us around the world are misguided and often tee me off. So the origin of my intense feelings for the USA can be charted back to those intense days in London. Throughout my year over there, I gave it to the America haters good, often using a very loud New Yawk accent to do my debating. Blimey.

To this day, I believe much of the anti-Americanism in Europe is driven by simple jealousy. America is a big, loud dog that generally struts its stuff. Many folks, even in the United States, do not like that kind of presentation. Overseas, some people form shallow, negative judgments about the USA without understanding or even looking at the overall picture. Throughout our history, Americans have freed hundreds of millions of people all over the world, yet a 2007 Pew Research poll, to use one example, found that the majority of British subjects have an unfavorable view of America. Even fueled by Guinness, that's a tough one to swallow.

About two months into my first semester in London, I got a bit bored with the rain and decided to see the rest of Europe. I bought a small motorcycle and set off. Before I was through, I had cut scores of classes but visited Ireland, Spain, Portugal, Morocco, France, Italy, Switzerland, Germany, Belgium, Holland, Denmark, Norway, Sweden, and Austria. Not to mention Andorra, Liechtenstein, Luxembourg, and San Marino. What an education!

Back then, the only continental country where I sensed a strong anti-American feeling was France. But I quickly learned the French don't like anyone. There's a story about President Johnson being so fed up with the anti-Americanism of Charles de Gaulle that he called the French president and threatened to exhume every American body buried in Normandy and ship the corpses back to the USA. I believe the story is true.

But some attitudes notwithstanding, traveling around Europe was a blast. As a history major, I couldn't get enough of it. From the Rhine castles to the Swiss Alps to the French Riviera, each destination was thrilling to a hometown guy like me, whose family vacation history was spelled V-E-R-M-O-N-T.

However, I did compare all the places I visited with home, and guess what? Home always won. Some will call it chauvinism, but for me the USA simply worked better. The socialism I saw in northern Europe sapped initiative and limited achievement. The fascism I saw in Franco's Spain was downright nasty. One of Franco's Guardia Civil goons actually awakened me on a train in the middle of the night by tapping my leg with a machine gun. My infraction: my foot was resting on the empty seat across from me.

Arriving in Germany, I found the communist wall dividing that country to be offensive and depressing. From my safe haven across the divide, I actually gave an East German guard the finger, something I rarely do.

So I got to see a lot of overseas stuff up close and personal, and all of it confirmed that the land of the free and the home of the brave was the perfect place for a working-class kid like me. When I visited Vatican City, I lit a candle in St. Peter's, thanking God I was born an American. And I believe many Italians would echo the sentiment.

Since my first adventure abroad, I have traveled extensively, visiting more than seventy countries. And always upon my return, when the U.S. customs agent says, "Welcome home," I get a chill. Every time.

Get Back Home, Loretta

Coming back to the USA to finish college in the fall of 1970 was something of a shock. The killing of four Kent State students by National Guardsmen in May of that year had radicalized millions more Americans against the war and the government. To my amazement, even the atmosphere at traditionalist Marist College had completely changed.

When I left for England, Marist was primarily a beer-drinking school. But in one year that image had evaporated. Pot, hashish, and LSD had replaced the kegs. Some of my friends who had haircuts like Dennis the Menace when I left now looked like one of the Kinks (British rock group, grooming challenged). Pampered white kids from Scarsdale were quoting Huey Newton, the "minister of defense" for the Black Panthers. As they said back then: "Far out."

For me, a budding independent thinker, most of this stuff was nonsense. Huey Newton? Please. "Power to the people"? Sure. Jane Fonda for secretary of state and Jimi Hendrix for president! The only thing I found fundamentally interesting about the Age of Aquarius was the change in attitude among many young women. See, sexual politics had hit Marist College hard. In the space of a year, sleeping with someone had gone from a fairly serious decision to "if it feels good, do it."

Of course, that philosophy, when it comes to substances, can easily lead to rehab or to the morgue, as Joplin, Hendrix, Morrison, and scores of others would amply demonstrate. But back in the fall of 1970, drug and dating protocols were "evolving," and it was fascinating to watch. Scrawny, unkempt guys who were lepers to the opposite sex just twelve months prior were now making out very well, especially if they spouted radical rubbish and had a stash of weed. To me, it was madness. To the nebbishes, it was heaven on earth.

Very simply, I was able to keep rather than "feed" my head, because I did not do drugs (again, we'll explore that later). I refused to join "Lucy in the Sky with Diamonds." I lost out on some, uh, social gratification for my stance, but I'm very glad I held the line. Also, I was busy enough with writing and football to avoid most "heavy" conversations (that's BS in today's lexicon). But I couldn't avoid the loud, pulsating Cream and Vanilla Fudge music, or the clouds of pot smoke on my dormitory floor. That was *really* annoying.

So although the mood on campus had turned far left, I couldn't "dig it." I wasn't conservative, but I wasn't grooving to the SDS (Students for a Democratic Society) either. Basically, I stayed out of the fray. I was back on the football team, writing for the paper, and counting the days until graduation. Crosby, Stills, Nash, and Young were asking me: "What if you knew her and found her dead on the ground?" But, perhaps selfishly, I was holding back on any answer.

In fact, the entire antiwar thing was numbing. Every day the same chant, the same rant. The only entertaining political thing that happened was Elvis visiting Nixon at the White House. On December 21, 1970, the King showed up on Pennsylvania Avenue looking like he had just partied with Willie Nelson. Nixon posed for a picture with the E-man, seemingly oblivious to the King's "state of mind."

I have that famous picture hanging on my office wall to this day.

But the gruesome hits just kept on coming. In the spring of 1971, Lt. William Calley was convicted of premeditated murder in the killings of twenty-two Vietnamese civilians at My Lai, effectively removing any semblance of the moral high ground from the American military effort. The world was seething at the United States, and things at Marist were getting out of control as well, with boycotts and demonstrations and sit-ins. Remember, this was regular-people Poughkeepsie, New York, not pseudointellectual Cambridge, Massachusetts. I couldn't keep up with the outrage du jour and didn't even try. I felt terrible for our troops in Vietnam because some of them were my friends and I knew they were good people. I understood that Calley was a criminal; I also knew he did not represent the vast majority of the American military. But my point of view was drowned out by the fierce antiwar frenzy on display everywhere.

Slowly, I grew to detest the excess and arrogance displayed by some of those antiwar people.

I speak from direct experience. One fine spring day, I was walking across campus heading for my French Hegemony class. Now, this course was not exactly a blast, but the professor, Peter O'Keefe, was a smart guy and aimed to present the material in a relevant way. So I showed up twice a week and tried to learn something about European history.

As I approached the classroom building, a long-haired guy, badly in need of shampoo and conditioner, blocked my way.

"Nobody's going to class today," he said. "We're having a 'solidarity' meeting."

"Enjoy it, bud," I shot back. "I'll see you over there."

"You can't go to class," the student insisted.

"I *can't?*"

"That's right, man, you can't."

I hate to admit this, because I don't relish physical confrontation, but I grabbed the guy, tossed him into some bushes, and proceeded along to my class. He weighed about eighty pounds, so it wasn't exactly World Wrestling Entertainment under way. However, the altercation left me more than a little steamed. There's a line you don't cross with me, and this minimilitant had crossed that line. It was my first brush with left-wing totalitarianism. There would be many more to come.

That day only four students showed up for class; the rest knew they had a valid excuse for cutting. Professor O'Keefe discussed the situation with us, putting forth the view that the dissenters, the antiwar "movement," brooked no dissent themselves. They had morphed into bitter, anti-American automatons whose actions were far more destructive than constructive.

I found that analysis interesting and generally on the mark. Although I have to say there were some very sincere antiwar people who did not despise their country and truly wanted peace for all. The "power to the people" crowd, however, generally overwhelmed those voices.

The rest of the semester played out peacefully enough, and in May I graduated with honors but, still, with little interest in politics. I followed the subsequent Vietnam peace talks, read the paper, and watched a little TV news. But for me, sports and friends still dominated my life.

As the war was winding down, I was looking ahead. Luckily, I got a job as a high school teacher in a poor suburb of Miami, Florida, and dialed into building a worthwhile life for myself in a country that allowed me to do so. Some of my college friends continued chasing Grace Slick's "White Rabbit," but not me. I wanted to do something good, and teaching seemed to be the pathway.

Politics, however, still hovered over my head a bit. As a history major, I was assigned to teach a course called Contemporary Problems, which would involve analysis of current events. In choosing the course readings, I decided to introduce both sides of the arguments and encourage students to think independently, not parrot the views of their peers or parents.

The class worked, and quickly became one of the most popular at Monsignor Edward Pace High School. Far from the left-wing indoctrination that dominated college campuses, my course examined the obvious problems in America, but always with a respectful overview that acknowledged the historical greatness of the country.

To this day, I have not deviated from that approach and believe it is a key to my success. Independent thinking leads to problem solving, fairness, compassion, and wisdom. Putting that discipline into practice helps me decide exactly where I stand on many subjects. Rejecting the so-called popular wisdom leads me to research my opinions and accumulate facts to back them up.

In contrast, Kool-Aid–drinking ideology, whether left or right, usually leads to narrow-mindedness, robotic acceptance of propaganda, and, eventually, embarrassment when the party line collapses, as it inevitably will in some cases. No ideology is correct on every issue.

So I'm real comfortable in the zone of independence. There, my traditional beliefs are accepted, and I serve no political master. I may be bold and fresh with this attitude, but I'm also free to see both sides of complicated situations and embrace solutions wherever I can find them.

It's a nice place to be.

CHAPTER

SELF-RELIANCE

You've been told, so maybe it's time that you learned.
—ERIC CLAPTON, "I CAN'T STAND IT"

One of the worst sights ever seen in America was the mass panic in New Orleans after Hurricane Katrina hit in 2005. You remember the scenes: thousands of people jumbled together in the dark, odoriferous Superdome without adequate food, water, or restroom facilities . . . families pleading for help from rooftops as muddy floodwaters rose, threatening their lives. Then, as the days dragged on, hundreds of exhausted survivors waiting under a scorching sun to be evacuated from highway overpasses.

This was America? All over the world folks were shocked when those awful scenes were broadcast on television. We expect to see these kinds of scenarios in Third World countries, but not from the richest, most technologically advanced nation on the planet. How could that happen in the land of plenty? Where was the swift, efficient assistance that many Americans expected?

Almost immediately after Katrina hit, the ideologues sprang into action. It was racial, the skin-color hustlers wailed. Most of those stranded were black and poor. America and George Bush don't care about them. Rapper Kanye West actually said that at a public appearance. Later, comedian Chris Rock told a political fund-raiser audience that Bush couldn't get to the California fires fast enough because "white people were burning," but the President had no time for the poor blacks in New Orleans. Rock then said Bush used "Katrina water" to douse the California flames.

Not to be outdone by a rapper and a comedian, left-wing loons in the media like *New York Times* columnist Paul Krugman blamed most of the Katrina misery on Mr. Bush. Over the years, the prevailing wisdom from the *Times*'s crew has been that Bush loathes the poor and wants to see them suffer. Thus, Bush stood by willfully as the New Orleans disaster unfolded. Here's part of what Krugman wrote:

> The federal government's lethal ineptitude wasn't just a
> consequence of Mr. Bush's personal inadequacy; it was a
> consequence of ideological hostility to the very idea of using
> government to serve the public good.

But the hysteria party was just getting started. Film director Spike Lee then offered an opinion that the levees in New Orleans might have been *intentionally* sabotaged to harm poor people of color.

Amid all this insanity, my take on the Katrina aftermath was pithy and blunt. Certainly some innocent poor people received cruel blows, and every American should have been sympathetic to their plight. And many of us were, as billions of charitable dollars flowed into the hurricane zone. But there was another huge factor in play as well.

A few days after the storm hit, I said this on television:

> There is no question the Bush administration was slow
> in getting relief to the hurricane zone. That's legitimate

criticism . . . (but) the truth is this: Governor Blanco of
Louisiana did not have a disaster plan in place, did not have
enough state police and National Guard to secure a city the
size of New Orleans, and did not push for federal help soon
enough.

New Orleans is not about race; it's about class. If you're
poor, you're powerless, not only in America but also
everywhere on earth. If you don't have enough money to
protect yourself from danger, danger is going to find you.
And all the political gibberish in the world is not going to
change that.

The aftermath of Hurricane Katrina should be taught in
every American school. If you don't get educated, if you
don't develop a skill and force yourself to work hard, you'll
most likely be poor. And sooner or later, you'll be standing
on a symbolic rooftop waiting for help.

Chances are that help will not be quick in coming.

In my opinion, that was one of my best TV commentaries ever.
But after I delivered it, the far-left Internet smear sites went into
spasms of indignation, rolling out headlines like:

O'REILLY BLAMES THE POOR FOR THE KATRINA DISASTER!

Syndicated columnist Liz Smith picked up the chatter and
wrote:

Fox News emperor Bill O'Reilly tells us in Katrina's wake
that if we—Americans—depend on the United States
government for any reason, we are certain to be disappointed.
Bill's advice to America (to the poor of New Orleans,
especially) is to educate yourself and get a well-paying job.
Only then can you avoid standing on a metaphorical rooftop

when the next disaster rolls around. Bill did not give the poor
any advice on how one finds a proper education or a job.
Remember, the government can't help.

Now, I like Liz Smith. She's a self-proclaimed liberal but a fair-
minded person who does much good for others. But, come on, Liz,
are there no schools where you live? You don't "find" a proper education; you work for one. Yes, some schools, especially in the poor
precincts, are inadequate despite record federal spending. But there
are kids in those schools who excel. And once children achieve a decent education, chances are they'll join the vast majority of Americans who have been able to secure a decent job.

Let's do some math. Each year, some ten million or more illegal
alien workers are able to earn billions of dollars in the U.S. economy and send much of that to their families back home. So what's
the lesson here? It's simple: I believe almost every American can
prosper if he or she does what is absolutely necessary. That is: learn
a skill, work hard. If that mantra were drummed into America's children, this country would be a far better place.

But don't tell that to the far left. Liberal thought, at times, allows
for people to avoid taking responsibility for their lives. If someone
fails to do the basics in order to succeed, it's not really their fault,
you see. It's callous society or the evil Bush administration that has
held them back. Liberal thought is very clear: the government has an
obligation to make sure all three hundred million Americans, plus
millions of illegal immigrants, have everything they need to get by.

That, of course, is unworkable nonsense, a kind of quasi-socialism
that, if embraced by an individual, will lead to disaster. America is
a capitalist nation, a place of intense competition. You have a better
chance of dating Britney Spears than you have of the feds making
sure your life is working out.

The Katrina debacle really disturbed me. I couldn't stop thinking
about it. Since I wanted my analysis of the situation to really mean

something, I began to investigate and talked to some of the folks who did not evacuate New Orleans ahead of the storm. Most admitted that they ignored the repeated warnings. Some said they had no money for a bus ticket out of town. Others told me they had nowhere to go, no family or friends outside the Big Easy. Even though I found those admissions startling, I believed them.

But, again, here's the lesson. If you have no money, no support system, no common sense, and no motivation to provide security for yourself and your family, you are going to get hammered. It's not a matter of *if*—it's a matter of *when*.

That said, there's no question but that the local, state, and federal governments screwed up after Katrina hit. Are you surprised? If you are, say hello to the Tin Man for me, because you are definitely living in the land of Oz. And when that house fell on the Wicked Witch after the tornado, did FEMA show up to help her? No, it did not. And Dorothy looted her ruby slippers!

So wise up fast or you'll lose your shoes too. Despite their impassioned rhetoric, the lefty pointy-heads at Harvard and in the media can't help you. When an administration promises that it will elevate your life and protect you on a personal level, you're being conned. The feds are good at collecting taxes and organizing the military. Aside from that, Washington is very limited in what it can actually achieve.

Bottom line: If you don't have loyal friends and family, you are on your own. "Read it, learn it, live it," as the guy said in *Fast Times at Ridgemont High*.

Wise Up Fast!

Looking back, the reason that I have succeeded in life is that I relied on myself, not on some mythical theory about government.

If I had lived in New Orleans, I would have gotten in my car and driven the hell out of there as soon as the National Weather Service gave warning. At no time would I have considered counting on Big Easy mayor Ray Nagin for anything. The man can barely figure out the lock on his office door. Same thing with Governor Kathleen Blanco and President Bush. I'm not counting on them for anything. Call me cynical.

Now, I really do feel sorry for the folks who did not or could not leave New Orleans. Using the resources of my program, we were able to get some of them evacuated and perhaps saved a few lives. I also said prayers for them. But there are Americans right now in the same spot as the hurricane victims were. They are either too dumb, too lazy, too mentally challenged, or too unlucky to have provided themselves with basic protections. So this chapter is dedicated to those who have little control over what happens to them in life. Hey, you guys, you can turn it around. Listen up.

Even when I was just five years old, I had to be somewhat self-reliant. That's because I attended Miss Dalton's kindergarten class at the Bowling Green public school. Basically, this campus was a free-for-all where we urchins ran wild. My friend Jimmy Cunningham and I, both junior hooligans, spent the days building things with blocks and then gleefully knocking down what we'd built. We were training to be Teamsters and didn't even know it. I'm surprised I didn't get a tattoo.

My point is that the teacher, Miss Dalton, exerted little control in the classroom and absolutely none on the playground. Routinely, kids wiped out on the steel monkey bars and smashed their small skulls on the concrete below. I mean it was survival of the fittest in every sense. There were no "playdates," bicycle helmets, or organized activities. It was demolition derby every day, and the kid with the most bruises won. Miss Dalton, with her mousy brown hair and thick glasses, wasn't much of a factor, so to speak. She was around—the pictures prove it—but there were few what I call "Barney" moments. In fact, had a singing purple dinosaur actually been introduced into the kindergarten fray back then, things might have turned ugly.

That kind of kid environment shapes you. Think about a five-year-old pioneer kid back in the nineteenth century. No "playdates" for those tykes, no sir; they were too busy shooting bears and watching for roaming Apaches. Back then a male child became a man at age thirteen and that was that. The young guy had to learn not only to survive, but also to protect his family. Nobody was waiting for President Grant to help out.

Survival of the fittest,
Levittown-style.

How things have changed. Today, the loony left is peddling the "nanny state," and millions of Americans are buying the idea. How ridiculous. How dangerous. It was quite the opposite when I was growing up in the huge, sprawling suburb of Levittown. There, self-reliance was a must. With literally hundreds of kids wandering around looking for action, conflict was everywhere. Every day, "rank-out" sessions took place. These verbal jousts were designed to diminish your opponent's "self-esteem." My favorite put-down was: "Your mother wears combat boots!" What the heck does that mean, anyway? Nobody quite knew. But it was big, and if you let loose with that rank-out, fists were likely to fly. In Levittown, moms were sacred.

There may not have been combat boots, but there was certainly combat itself. And God help any boy who ran home to Mom or Dad for assistance or sympathy. He immediately became a leper. I mean, there were serious consequences for getting Ozzie or Harriet involved in your conflicts. The kids generally settled stuff themselves. Nobody had money for a lawyer.

Not that any parent wanted to get dragged into that stuff. My father's orders—and I can still hear him bellowing—were to "come home when the streetlights come on and don't take any garbage from your idiot friends." That was it, and he didn't want to hear about the gory details. My father could not have cared less what went on in Toyland.

This is not to say that everybody in my neighborhood turned out to be self-reliant; they did not. My earliest friends were Johnny, Charlie, and Larry (names are changed). We started playing together at four years old. Eventually, two of them grew up to become drug addicts; Johnny actually died from AIDS in his early forties, breaking his mother's heart. Larry signed up for Scientology. So early reliance on self is not an indicator of a happy life, but for me the school of hard knocks worked. Never did I expect the cavalry to rush to my rescue. I fought my own battles, won more than I lost, and developed a cocky attitude that continues to serve me well. If I wanted money, I worked for it. If I wanted to play football, I organized a game. Life was simple: You want it—make it happen. Somebody bothers you; deal with it.

Watch and Learn

There was another reason that self-reliance showed up early in my life: my father's job. Over the years I watched my dad surrender his dignity to the Caltex oil company. He knew that his mundane accounting job did not challenge his potential. He told me so on his deathbed. After a while, the slow drip, drip, drip of daily boredom drove my father kind of crazy. Every day, he would get up and go to a job he hated. Imagine living that kind of life.

My father did not seek a better alternative because, frankly, he was scared (we'll deal with fear in the next chapter). Being raised during the Great Depression, when jobs were scarce and despair was in the air, caused him and many others to believe that economic doom was always hiding in the closet, just waiting to pounce. So as long as his meager paycheck kept coming, he would tough it out and not look for something better.

Some of my father's superiors at Caltex sensed his weakness and, as a result, treated him badly, which, of course, was hard to swallow for a guy like him. Eventually, the frustration he felt affected his health. Still, he did not take action. Year after year passed without advancement. Tragically, he depended on a corporate giant that could not have cared less about him. Finally, after thirty-five years, Caltex gave him a cheap watch and a small pension. See ya.

After watching that situation up close and personal, no way was I ever going to rely on any company, government, or person. I was your standard-issue dopey kid, but I absorbed one thing: I was going to make money and forge a career on my own terms. No fear. I would continue being a bold, fresh piece of humanity, and *blank* anyone who didn't like it.

One of the great things about America is that we are allowed to fall flat on our faces, as Vince Lombardi pointed out, but then get back up and try again. I believe that this is the key that turns the good-life lock.

My father had a college education and did work hard. But many times, that's not enough. My dad never took a chance. Like the New Orleans people who refused to move in the face of a vicious oncoming storm, my father hunkered down and got clobbered. No one came to help.

If there is only one thing that you take from this book, let it be this: Design your own life. Never give up trying to make it on your own. Get back up when you get slapped down, and don't waste time buying into ideological nonsense. Expect—and accept—nothing from anyone else. Do it yourself.

And, after you have succeeded, share some of what you've achieved with those not as strong as you will become. That's important. Spread the self-reliance message, but also help good people when they need a hand.

Once in a while, on my radio program, a caller will kid around about all the money I make and say something like: "Hey, send me some of that."

And I say: "You wouldn't take it, would you?"

Usually, that rates a pause on the line. The caller is thinking about something that he or she hasn't heard before: *Well, why wouldn't I take it?* The answer, again, is simple: If you earn it, it'll mean a lot more than if it's given to you. Taking stuff makes you weaker. Earning stuff makes you stronger.

That's Right, Jack!

One of my favorite actors is Jack Nicholson, a true American original. Even if the movie he's in is a dog, Nicholson finds some way to elevate his role. The guy is creative and daring and outrageous.

So I wasn't surprised to read in *Parade* magazine that Nicholson made it on his own. His father abandoned him; he did not find out until he was thirty-seven years old that the woman he knew as his older sister was really his mother. His grandmother had pretended to be his mother. "From age 11," he told *Parade*, "I had to make my own money working. It was an advantage, because I always knew that, whatever I did, I'd have to do it on my own."

Even though I was lucky enough to have two loving parents, I started earning money even earlier than Nicholson. In Levittown there were two big job opportunities for urchins: grass cutting and snow shoveling.

Early on, my father had a manual lawn mower; you pushed it and grass got cut. In the middle of a hot, humid August, this was slave labor, and few adults wanted to do it. So dopey kids did it. In 1960, I got a buck a lawn. Gathering up the clippings was fifty cents extra.

Then my father splurged for a "power mower." The problem here, as some of you will remember, was getting the damn thing to start. You had to pull a tightly coiled starter rope with a wicked snap. Most kids were too weak to kick the thing into gear. It was maddening. Also, you had to put gas into the mower, and I usually spilled the fuel, making me a potential human torch. Sometimes my father helped me out with the mower, but often he was not around. But once up and running, the power mower was faster and far easier than the push mower; however, there always seemed to be complications with the contraption. Nevertheless, I had about five lawns a week, and the cash kept me in movie and candy money, with a little left over for the Good Humor ice-cream guy.

Shoveling snow was a much better deal. Just a steel shovel and your back muscles. Two friends and I could knock off ten driveways before lunch. A buck a driveway, plus many of the Levittown moms would throw in a mug of hot chocolate and cookies. Perks!

Back then before Al Gore caused global warming (just a jest for you far-left nuts), it snowed in New York consistently for three months. So, from the time I was nine to age sixteen, the snow economy was brilliant for me. I bought my Willie Mays–model Mac-Gregor baseball glove with snow money, and I still use it today!

Snow was a moneymaking occasion—
back when it actually snowed.

By the way, try asking most kids to shovel snow today. You'll get some very interesting facial expressions.

When I was sixteen, when it became legal to do so, I got a so-called real job at a Carvel ice-cream stand. This was primo. Basically, I got paid for eating ice cream and, occasionally, dishing it out. Since the guy who owned the store, Frank N., was rarely around, the inmates definitely ran the asylum. We knew Frank expected a couple of hundred bucks a day from sales, and we delivered for him. But, at the same time, we were not exactly the "customer is always right" type guys.

Here's what I mean. Every couple of days, one very large woman would drive up to the Carvel stand in her fine white Cadillac. Moments later, a pudgy little kid, most likely her son, would saunter up to the service window to order ice cream. On just about every occasion, the kid would screw up the order and the lady would then alight from her car, laying on the attitude. Sometimes she went ballistic over butterscotch topping; other times there was not enough hot fudge to suit her.

Since we didn't care, we'd listen to the tirade and generally mock the woman. One time, I asked her nicely (I swear) if, perhaps, a five-year-old might not be the best option for placing the order. She told me to mind my own business.

Okay.

One August night, Bangladesh hot and humid, the zaftig woman drives up, the little kid gets out of the car, and he predictably waddles over with his order. "One hot-fudge sundae with extra hot fudge," he squeaks, "one chocolate cone with sprinkles."

Okay.

So the best employee in Carvel history, me, whips up the sundae and then piles the cone high with soft chocolate ice cream. And I mean high. Straight up high, so there was no base upon which the ice cream could rest. The cone was straight as a pencil.

We, the highly trained, ultraprofessional Carvel staff, then watched from inside the store as the little kid slowly walked back toward the white Caddy, both his hands filled to capacity. Almost immediately the cone began to wobble, the ice cream slowly swaying in the humid breeze.

Taking in the scene from behind the wheel, the offending woman's eyes widened. She realized the calamity that was quickly unfolding before her. She opened the door, but her bulk prevented a swift exit. Then gravity took over. The cone swayed one last time and, almost in slow motion, the dark brown frozen cream fell, landing on the hood of her shiny automobile. Splat! Did I mention the car was white?

The child, distraught and panic-stricken, then dropped the sundae, and all that "extra" hot fudge hit the steamy, sticky pavement, immediately finding a comfortable home.

Appalled, the large lady sprinted to the window demanding a refund. I told her she was lucky I didn't charge her for the parking-lot cleanup (certainly that was bold and fresh). She continued to yell, demanding to see the manager. Since I was that person, an unkind smirk crossed my mouth. Finally, she left in a major snit. Another satisfied customer.

My Carvel experience lasted about two years. I averaged about a buck-forty and twenty laughs an hour. But then it was time to move up in the employment world. Using my swimming prowess, and armed with a water-safety instructor card, I convinced the Town of Babylon on Long Island to kindly pay me two-fifty an hour to teach little kids to swim. How can you hate that?

Quick story. One hot summer day I had finished my morning swim class at the pool and was sauntering around trying to look cool just in case there were some girls my age in the vicinity. The young ladies were not happening, but there were dozens of children splashing around and, just by chance, I looked down into the water. There at the bottom of the pool was a little kid staring up at me. And he wasn't moving. My instincts kicked in fast: I jumped into the water, which was about eight feet deep, grabbed the kid's arm, and hauled him up. Upon breaking the water's surface, the kid began to cry and spit out liquid, lots of liquid. His mother came running over and thanked me profusely. The little boy was shaken but fine. I was proud of myself.

About thirty-three years later, I was signing copies of my book *The No Spin Zone* at a store on Long Island. A man walked up to the table and said, "Thanks for saving my life." What? Incredibly, it was the kid. He told me his mom had never forgotten the incident or the name of the teenager who had pulled her son out of the water. And after I had achieved some fame, the mother told her son the pool story. Is that amazing or what?

Teaching swimming was rewarding, and fairly good money at the time for a high school student, but those wages weren't going to cut it during college. I needed better money to be able to put gas in my car and go out on an occasional date, although that was wishful thinking most of the time. So, after some deliberation, I decided to start a house-painting business. As many teenagers say today: Oh . . . my . . . God!

The Color Purple

It was the beginning of summer, 1968, and things were not going well. Vietnam was raging and the economy was soft. Richard Nixon and Hubert Humphrey were getting ready to slug it out in the presidential contest, but few of us in Levittown cared about that. We were all trying to earn some decent money, and it wasn't easy.

Some of my friends signed on at the McDonald's on Old Country Road, but I resisted. The money was terrible, and when those guys finished their shifts, they smelled like French fries. There had to be a better way.

One fine day, a friend's mother, disgusted that we were hanging around looking like slobs and doing nada, suggested we paint her house. I believe I said something stupid like, "Is Tom Sawyer not available?"

But paint her house we did. And she gave us a hundred dollars each. By Carvel standards that was about sixty-five hours of work. And even though we horsed around a great deal, we finished the project in about three days, about twenty-four hours of labor. My dim mind calculated that we had each made just short of five bucks an hour. Gold mine.

Originally, the houses in Levittown were small and coated with slatelike shingles: in other words, very little wood trim. The dwellings were easy to paint, even for boobs like us. Unfortunately, there was one major downside to developing a lucrative painting franchise: few in Levittown had any money, so homeowners usually painted their houses themselves or ignored the situation until their neighbors threatened to firebomb.

But, with some clever marketing, I was able to secure a few exterior painting jobs. One problem: I really didn't know what I was doing. Customers would ask me about caulking and scraping and priming, and I would say, "Of course." In reality, I had no clue.

So I went to see my friend the Bear, a big guy whom I had known since the first grade. The Bear said very little, ate plenty, and would sleep through the winter if you'd let him. That's why, to this day, he is still called the Bear.

Anyway, the Bear knew a little about painting but was not interested in actually doing it. That's because he had a great job as a janitor in a grocery store, where he cleaned up incredibly gross stuff for two-fifty an hour. His shift was midnight to eight a.m. I mean, how could you leave that?

I told the Bear in no uncertain terms that he was a moron and that he would make huge money painting homes with me in the daylight hours. Unfortunately, the Bear *was* a moron on many occasions, and this was one of them.

But I needed the guy. So, finally, I took my appeal to the Bear's father, Fred. A tightfisted man of German descent, Fred had five other smaller bears at home eating him out of said dwelling. I bluntly told Fred that the Bear was passing up about two hundred bucks a week, off the books.

The next day, armed with a used paintbrush, the Bear showed up at my house.

For the next five summers we painted hundreds of houses and made more than ten thousand dollars each. This was enormous money at the time. We worked hard, but nobody was telling us what to do. We called the shots—it was our business.

In fact, things became so lucrative, we had so much work, that we actually had to hire some of the neighborhood guys in order to complete all the contracts. This is where things got dicey, because most of the neighborhood guys made the Bear look like a brain surgeon.

Trust me, I tried to keep things simple. All the guys had to do was slap paint on shingles and wood trim, making sure the paint did not get on anything else. We never used oil-based paint, because that stuff is like a roadside bomb: at any moment you can die from inhaling it. We used latex paint from Sears. It was smooth, easy to apply, and glowed upon application.

All the neighborhood guys were under strict instructions to put drop cloths underneath wherever they were painting. That way, when some paint did inevitably fall to the ground, it would hit the cloth and not damage anything. Because of the intricacy of this concept, I explained it many times using actual drop cloths in my presentation. Most of the guys got it. One did not.

As I related in my book *The O'Reilly Factor for Kids,* the culprit was Jeff Cohen. Late one afternoon Cohen was high on a ladder painting away. Then, in one motion, he dropped his paint can. It should have hit his drop cloth but it did not. Because no drop cloth was laid out beneath him.

Instead, Cohen's white paint splattered all over a very green bush, a nice bush, a bush that sat in front of the house alongside other very nice bushes. This was not good.

Quickly, I threw a drop cloth over the now white bush to hide the catastrophe. After cursing Cohen, I calmly assessed the situation. There was no substance on earth that could remove the paint from the foliage without killing it; that was number one. Second, to buy a new bush would take much of the job money, because we worked cheap. Third, the owner of the house was not an understanding kind of guy, if you know what I mean. If the man found out we had murdered the bush, even accidentally, full payment for the job might have been in jeopardy.

Faced with those facts, I could do only one thing. Late that same night, Cohen and I returned to the house, removed the cloth covering the white bush, and quietly sawed that sucker down. This, of course, left a major hole in the foliage. We then went to some nearby woods, gathered up a little foliage, and brought it back, placing it strategically around the missing bush. Obviously, a desperate and ridiculous patch job.

When we completed the paint job a couple of days later, I walked around the house with Mr. Jenkins (not his real name). The fresh paint looked great, but the man kept staring at the front of the dwelling.

"Something looks different," the guy said.

"You know, Mr. Jenkins, everybody says that after their house is painted. It's a natural reaction."

I had rehearsed that in my mind before saying it.

"Guess so."

I cashed his check within minutes.

Like my student year abroad, the painting business was a turning point in my life. Create your own opportunities and execute them. Rely on no one else when it comes to improving your situation. As Home Depot says today: "You can do it. We can help."

And here's the kicker to this ramble down memory lane: Exactly twenty-seven years after creating a painting business, I created *The O'Reilly Factor.* Even though I had a job in television at the time, I knew it wasn't good enough, that I could do better, and I did. (I'll explain how that all happened later on.)

One final thing in this chapter: like my friend the Bear, most people on this earth are reluctant to take chances, to improve their lives, to escape a stifling situation like my father endured for his entire working life. The big reason that many folks accept the unacceptable and settle for less than they can achieve can be summed up in one word: fear.

FEAR

Fear is your friend if you can control it.

—CUS D'AMATO, FAMED BOXING TRAINER

For my friend Lenny's seventh birthday, his parents took five of his hooligan friends, including the bold, fresh guy, to see a double feature: *Attack of the Crab Monsters* and *Not of This Earth*. These cheapie monster movies were made for about thirty-two dollars by the legendary American International Pictures under the hilarious supervision of a man named Roger Corman, who was known as King of the Bs.

The year was 1957. *Leave It to Beaver* had just debuted on television, Elvis had a smash hit with "Jailhouse Rock," and *The Bridge on the River Kwai* won the Oscar for Best Picture. *Attack of the Crab Monsters* did not come in second.

I vividly remember that day because it was the first time adults took us kids to see monsters in the cinema (British expression). Before that, we were restricted to mostly Disney stuff, and even though he is eternally young, Peter Pan was getting kind of old.

The birthday boy, Lenny, was a first-rate dolt, totally out of con-

trol and dim to boot. Everybody in the neighborhood—and believe
me, we are not talking Ph.D. candidates here—understood that
Lenny would be lucky to get out of the fifth grade.

But if Lenny's parents were paying, we were going and, as I remember, the first few minutes of *Crab Monsters* were a bit spooky.
That's because the actual creatures never appeared on-screen. That
exposition came later. In the beginning of the movie, you just heard
clicking sounds somewhere off in the dark jungle on a deserted
South Pacific island. The sound effects brought to mind very agitated crickets. It was eerie and menacing.

Then somebody on the island suddenly disappeared. Then, a few
minutes later, you heard the voice of the guy who had just vanished calling one of his pals. Then *that* guy went missing. We kids were spooked.

But not for long. When the crab monsters did finally show up, they looked like Mardi Gras parade floats. Five seven-year-olds hooted and mocked those monsters, even though radiation from bomb tests had made them huge and hungry. Not that we cared, but the movie was actually relevant. In 1954, the United States set off its biggest H-bomb test blast ever, and three real Pacific islands were vaporized.

But we kids weren't concerned about "no stinkin' radiation" and paused in our mocking only when one of the crab monsters decapitated a guy and swallowed his head. That was pretty neat and explained how the monsters could talk like people. Somehow, the voice box of the dearly departed kept on working inside the creature so that it could speak and knew what to say! Wow! It took us a few minutes to digest that (sorry), and then we began hooting again.

Attack of the Crab Monsters earned five thumbs down, and after a few coming attractions, the second film began. But this flick was a far different story. Filmed in stark black-and-white, *Not of This Earth* told the tale of an alien who came to earth and drained humans of blood. Unlike Dracula, however, the guy didn't drink the blood for nourishment. Carrying a little kit, he hypnotized victims with his strange eyes and then inserted a needle in a vein. The blood flowed into tubes he kept in a suitcase until it was all collected. Gross. Nobody said a word. This was scary stuff.

Wearing dark glasses to hide his weird eyes, the alien guy hunted down a variety of adults and eventually wound up chasing Beverly Garland all over the place. He *really* wanted Beverly's blood, and she wasn't happy about it. Finally, the good guys came to rescue Beverly, but somehow the aliens were not wiped out when the movie ended. In little-kid world, this was not good. Blood-seeking aliens at large could show up again, especially late at night in your dark room!

I remember most of the kids were petrified. Nobody said a word as we stumbled out of the theater. I can still see that alien guy in my mind to this day. The actor who played him was Paul Birch. I actu-

Is this a blood-guzzling alien or an anchorman on VENUS TV?

ally looked that up when I got older. *Not of This Earth* was a *serious* monster film, and although no one admitted it, I suspect some nightmares took place among my friends.

Despite that unsettling experience, I loved those movies. Few of them actually frightened me, but just the expectation of fear was exciting. My younger sister was just the opposite. She would *never* go to see those films, because, like most normal people, she found fear disturbing. But, somehow, I could not get enough of crazy monsters-and-horror mayhem. Every scary movie was a challenge.

War, Children, It's Just a Shot Away

To this day, I believe in confronting fears, from the imaginary to the very real and dangerous. We are all afraid at times—it's normal—but as the legendary boxing trainer Cus D'Amato pointed out, fear can be a powerful motivator. True courage is not about being fearless; it's about overcoming fear, going ahead with something worthwhile even though you're terrified.

The first time I faced a TV camera, as a reporter in Scranton, Pennsylvania, I was afraid of screwing up. But I never gave in to the fear. Even though I was downright awful during my first few weeks on the air, I persisted. And, after every on-camera appearance, I got better and mentally stronger. I overcame the fear. It was not so different from sitting through *Not of This Earth*.

As I progressed as a news reporter, the fear factor ratcheted up. The first time I entered a war zone, I did get a bit spooked. It was El Salvador, 1981, and as the Air Florida plane from Miami dropped out of the clouds, I looked out the window and saw tanks ringing the San Salvador airport. This was not a movie set. Less than two hours prior, I had been safe in south Florida. Now all that had changed. Real war, guns, and death lay before me. It was sobering, to say the least.

But, again, I relished the challenge and banished the fear from my mind. When the CBS News bureau chief asked for volunteers to check out an alleged massacre in the dangerous Morazán territory, a mountainous region bordering Nicaragua, I willingly went. And I'll freely admit it was damn frightening in those heavily forested mountains, with all kinds of armed bad guys roaming around and no law in sight. But I learned a tremendous amount about the conflict and about myself. I could face a high-risk situation. It was a huge confidence builder.

However, I should tell you one very important thing: I was never stupid. I never took foolish chances. I did my job and calculated the safety factor all the time. Once in a while, I made a mistake. But, generally, I kept my head down when the soot hit the fan, as it occasionally did.

In my novel *Those Who Trespass,* I vividly describe a TV news correspondent's near-death experience while covering the Falkland

Islands war in Argentina. Coincidentally, this bold, fresh piece of
humanity was also in that country during that conflict. Suffice it
to say that after nearly getting my head blown off in Buenos Aires
during a riot in front of the presidential palace, I gained a new ap-
preciation for life and an even greater hatred for corruption.

The Argentine action didn't stop me, though, from going to Northern Ireland at the height of the troubles, or to the Golan Heights, the
disputed territory that Israel and Syria are quarreling over. I've always been curious about world conflict and what really happens in
violent places. In fact, one of the best stories I've ever assembled
had to do with the Viet Cong tunnels underneath the hamlet of Chu
Chi outside Saigon.

In the summer of 1992, I traveled to Vietnam to interview a communist soldier who lived underground in those tunnels for two years.
For the TV segment, I intercut his story with that of an American
soldier, a so-called tunnel rat who hunted the VC in those dark cav-
erns. It was a riveting scenario: the ultimate cat-and-mouse chase.
Each man was trying to survive by killing the enemy, who was in
close proximity. Twenty-five years after the fact, both men told me
they still had terrifying nightmares. After hearing their stories, I understood that, compared to their ordeals, any fear I've had to face
pales in comparison.

Vietnam in the early 1990s was not a dangerous place. But, by
traveling through the hot, humid, dense, jungle-dominated country-
side, I could clearly sense just how that conflict had spiraled out of
control. In South Vietnam, the U.S. military could not tell friend
from foe, and it must have been maddening. It is similar, in several
ways, to the situations in Iraq and Afghanistan today: terrorists attacking while wearing civilian clothing and hiding behind noncom-
batants. They even use children as shields.

As you may know, I have visited both of those war zones. Some
people thought I was nuts to go, especially to Iraq in 2006, when

things were really nasty. But these days, I have a fatalistic attitude about danger, so fear never entered into my mind. It's my job to see for myself what I am talking and writing about when I can possibly do so. Besides, the U.S. military took great care of us in both places. In El Salvador there was no American military presence, so I had no protection at all. In light of that experience, my recent trips to war zones have been relatively stress-free.

The Eternal Struggle

Why am I telling you all this? Because I believe that overcoming fear is an essential key to living a useful and honorable life. Taming fear also trains a person to stand up to injustice. This is very important. When it is all over, when you are dead in the ground or in an urn, your legacy will be defined by two simple questions: How many wrongs did you right, and how many people did you help when they needed it?

That's it. Nothing more. No one will care how much money you made or what kind of car you drove. Those things don't inspire memorable eulogies.

So you can go ahead and hose people all day long, amassing great wealth and power, but what, exactly, does that mean? Nada, that's what. Note to the greed-heads and evildoers: you may be remembered for your misdeeds, but only as objects of ridicule or revulsion. On the other hand, the person who makes things better in this world will not be easily forgotten; his or her legacy will likely carry on. The good that you do in your life remains in the world.

But make no mistake: to attempt to right wrongs means conflict, and you will suffer. Most people are afraid of that suffering, so most people sit it out. My father was a role model in this regard, a good man afraid to stand up.

My core belief, as stated in my book *Culture Warrior,* is that life is a constant struggle between good and evil. That each person has free will and must choose a side. Refusing to choose puts one in the evil category by default, because bad things will then go unchallenged. The German people during the Nazi era demonstrated this better than anyone else. Most Germans were not Nazis, but most stood by and allowed incredible atrocities because they were either afraid or apathetic. Then they were forced to defend those atrocities by fighting World War II. Germany is still branded by that disgrace to this day.

But most evil is not as obvious as the work of Hitler and his pals, who flat out told the folks they were murderous racists. No, most bad people, out of cowardice or self-interest, attempt to disguise their evil. Some get justice, but some do not. For me, that's the most frustrating part of life: seeing evil individuals continue to harm people with impunity.

That's why I created the *Factor,* to hold those people accountable. To make sure that child rapists serve decades in prison, to expose judges who allow violent convicted felons to walk free, to call for aggressive action against terrorists who slaughter women and children. If you watch me on television, you know I am deeply invested in those things, and in the following chapter we'll specifically address the battle against evil in America and abroad.

But here's a fascinating subplot: some folks think *I* am the evil guy. If you don't believe me, just check out some of those loony extremist Web sites—there are plenty of people who hate me and would hurt me if they could.

Unfortunately, I mean that literally. My job commenting on life, liberty, and the pursuit of happiness has led to constant threats against me and, on a few occasions, against my family. This is where confronting fear comes in. These threats come in a variety of ways and are disconcerting, to say the least. One guy was actually sent to jail for stuff he did to me. This kind of garbage is, by far, the worst part of my life.

Going into detail about those threats serves no purpose here. But you should know that some very powerful people have encouraged that kind of vile activity, have encouraged people to harm me. We know who those people are, and I intend to deal with them sooner or later. Not a threat, a promise. Obviously, the struggle is intense, and if I weren't emotionally equipped to deal with fear, I could never do what I do every day. Not bragging, just stating.

There is no question that it would be far easier for me to do what most other TV people do: that is, go to work, let other people write and produce the program, and stay away from hot issues. I could make a nice living doing that, but I'd be bored stupid.

Some will call me delusional, but I truly believe that I was put on this earth for a reason and confronting evil is that purpose. At the risk of sounding self-righteous, I want to quote evil guy Hyman Roth who, when speaking to Michael Corleone in *Godfather II,* dismissed the dangers of Mafia life with a pithy summation: "This is the business we've chosen."

When you strip it all down, that's what I choose to do with my media power: expose bad guys. But, obviously, the bad guys don't like that and will do what bad guys do: that is, try to hurt you.

Now, sometimes, I make a wrong call on assessing evil but, fortunately, not too often. Before we go after someone, my staff does intense research, and a producer always calls the person in question to hear his or her side of the story. The *Factor* has been on the air for more than twelve years. We have never lost a court case and have never had to retract a story. When we make a factual mistake, we correct it as quickly as possible. But we never, ever back away from a story or an opinion because we're afraid it will lead to conflict. We embrace the challenge.

Hit 'Em Again, Harder, Harder

Two more stories on the subject of fear. First, in the late fall of 1967, I was a freshman at Marist College, one of three first-year guys to make the football team. In the music world, the Doors were just breaking through to the other side, *Cool Hand Luke* was failing to communicate in the movies, and *The Flying Nun,* with actress Sally Field, was soaring to the top on television.

On the field, I was a bit like Paul Newman's Luke character on the prison farm. I was getting pounded. Each week in practice, the third-stringers ran the plays of the opposing team so that the first string could see what might happen on game day. I, the bold, fresh guy, was the quarterback of the third team. The problem here was this: FULL CONTACT. That meant the third-stringers were going up against the first team as if we were playing a regular game. No "red shirt" on the quarterback so he wouldn't get hit. No, sir, I got smashed just like everybody else.

Gen. George Armstrong Custer would understand.

One very cold late November evening, the Marist Vikings were practicing at Riverview Field in Poughkeepsie, New York, preparing to play a night game the following Friday. The numbing wind whipped off the frigid Hudson River; the ground was as hard as Dick Cheney's heart; in short, the entire atmosphere was one of pure misery.

Predictably, such conditions teed everybody off. But one part of the team had an outlet for their frustrations: the first-team defense. If they wanted they could take the third-team quarterback, me, and the running backs apart limb by limb. Unfortunately, that evening, they wanted.

A mutiny was under way inside my huddle. The opposing first-string defensive Goliaths outweighed my offensive linemen by about a ton. Upon receiving a handoff, my running backs would simply fall down, correctly assessing that humiliation was better than de-capitation. All I had left was the pass. God help me.

At this point, I should tell you that in addition to being a quar-terback, I was also the punter and placekicker on the team. And I know this is hard to believe, but I was somewhat cocky on the field. In fact, just like my idol, Joe Namath of the New York Jets, I wore white cleats. It didn't matter that Namath had more football talent in his shoelaces than I had in my entire body; I still wore those shoes.

Some of the bigger, meaner guys on the Marist team did not quite understand the shoes, if you know what I mean.

That's me on the far right. Note the Namath number and white cleats.

Anyway, back to the cold, bleak, Stalingrad-like practice. Our coach, Ron Levine, admired guys like Darryl Royal and Bear Bry-ant, legendary college coaches who embraced brutal practices. So, a test of wills began to emerge. I, being bold and fresh, was not going to show the first team any fear or weakness. That was not going to happen.

Of course, given the circumstances, my attitude was beyond dumb. The entire third team was one *big* weakness. We were terrible. If we were any good, we would have been playing on the first team, right? Apparently, everybody knew this but me.

Realizing that the running game was nonexistent, I began calling pass plays. The problem was, I got hammered exactly three seconds after taking the snap from the center. Sometimes, I actually threw the ball in that short period of time. But it really didn't matter. No way were my receivers going to catch anything, primarily because their average height was five feet five inches.

So, time after time, I threw the ball and got slammed to the turf. Always, I sprang back up and snarled stupid stuff at the defense like, "Is that all you got?" Genius.

At that point, I should have been placed under psychiatric care. Any responsible institute of higher learning would have ordered that. But I was not given the head help I so obviously needed. Instead, I toughed out the practice and walked off the field under my own power, numb from the part in my hair on down.

After that pathetic display, a few of the first-teamers actually came up to me and mumbled stuff like, "Nice job." But then an incredible thing happened. The defensive coach, a crusty guy named Bill Linnehan, who rarely spoke to the leprous third string, stopped at my locker, stared at me for a second, and kept it pithy: "You may not be smart, O'Reilly, but you got guts."

Okay.

Taking that kind of beating way back then actually helped me in life. Every year, I get together with some of the defensive guys who pounded me into pudding. They usually bring up the frigid, brutal practice, and we have some laughs about it. After more than forty years, walking off that field remains a source of pride for me. Even though I was insane.

The final story about fear happened on January 5, 2008. I was up in New Hampshire covering the presidential primary when something very unexpected happened. My Fox News crew and I were stationed behind a short barrier waiting for a campaigning Barack Obama to walk by. I was hoping to get one question to the candidate.

All at once, a huge guy wearing an Obama jacket walked over and stood directly in front of my cameraman, blocking any shot he might have had. The shooter quickly moved a few feet to the left; the guy moved also, continuing to intentionally block the shot.

I then asked the guy to move, telling him he was interfering with our work. But he did not move. Because Obama was just seconds from passing us, I made the decision to move the guy myself. So I pushed him out of the way with precision. Did I mention he was six feet eight inches tall?

We later learned that the guy was a committed left-wing zealot. Not surprisingly, the incident made national news with some pinhead commentators actually calling me a bully. Sure. Too Tall Jones was the innocent victim. I love the media.

Even some of my Fox colleagues looked askance at my removal effort. But I'd do it again in a heartbeat. No one is going to do that to me. Ever. And the truth is that I never even thought about a reaction from the big guy; I guess he could have slugged me. But in my mind, he was going to move one way or another, and whatever happened, happened. No fear.

Get a Patton on It

While preparing to invade Sicily in 1943, Gen. George Patton issued a list of twenty-seven tactical adages to his commanders. One of them stated: "Never take counsel of your fears."

Simply put, Patton was acknowledging that every human being, even hardened military personnel, is afraid at times, but a leader cannot give in to fear, cannot allow it to dictate behavior or alter thinking.

That adage should be taught in every American school. Alas, in our soft and disturbingly selfish society, it never will be. Puts too much pressure on the kids, you see. But to make a difference in this world, to right wrongs and to truly combat evil, you must never let your fears control you. You don't have to be in the military or be an obnoxious TV commentator like some bold, fresh guy we know. In your own life, you can slap down fear by following Nancy Reagan's advice and just saying no to it.

Patton and most other great American leaders understood that. Now, hopefully, so do you.

CHAPTER 4

EVIL

No one knows about the times you've had,
You've been so evil, you've been so bad,
There's the devil to pay for what you've put them through,
And you've got a feeling somebody's following you.

—EAGLES, "SOMEBODY"

My definition of evil, like just about everything else about me, is simple and straightforward: If you knowingly hurt another human being without significant cause, like self-defense, you are committing an evil act. And if you do this as a matter of course, you *are* evil.

As I've noted in *Culture Warrior,* some people do not acknowledge evil at all. For them, it doesn't exist. They always come up with some excuse, some rationalization to explain away destructive behavior. Folks who embrace the secular-progressive philosophy often tend to believe that individual pursuits and desires are justification enough to harm people. That is, if someone is standing in the way of your personal gratification, then you can hurt that person with impunity.

That, I hope you'll agree, is an evil way to think.

If you don't believe me, ask my third-grade teacher, the afore-mentioned Sister Mary Lurana, who was an expert on evil if there ever was one. I mean, this woman had it *down.* The good sister knew every variation of the Ten Commandments, and I doubt that anyone else in the history of Christianity has ever found so many subtexts in them. According to scripture, Moses was given just two stone tablets on Mount Sinai. Somehow, Sister Lurana's scholarship had expanded the tablet dictums so that even Moses himself might have been a little confused. We'll get into that in the next chapter.

For now, however, let's take a look at our popular culture and make some judgments (alert the secular-progressives). I'll ask the questions; you provide the answers as you see fit.

Query #1: As you may know, some rap lyrics glorify drugs, both selling and using. Also, the many irresponsible rappers make it look cool to use violence against women, gays, and just about everybody else. On more than a few occasions, rap and hip-hop have advocated a totally disrespectful view of human life.

According to many teachers and child psychologists, these explicit rap songs can, and do, negatively influence some children, especially those from chaotic families. So, in the land of the free, are the people who profit from this activity doing evil?

Query #2: Torture movies are flooding the market, especially in the summer, when young people are looking for something to do. These cynical films revel in explicit scenes of human suffering inflicted with a cavalier glee by both the actors and the special-effects people. Sadism rules, and some sociologists believe a diet of this stuff desensitizes people, making them less likely to sympathize with the real-life suffering of others. So, are the people profiting from torture movies evil?

Query #3: Child abuse is epidemic in America; that means millions of defenseless kids are harmed in dreadful ways. Not surprisingly, studies show conclusively that much of the abuse and neglect is the result of persistent intoxication on the part of parents or guardians. Are child abusers evil even if they have a substance problem?

Query #4: Terrorists around the world are responsible for killing and injuring hundreds of thousands of human beings. Are all terrorists evil?

Query #5: Hundreds of Catholic priests have been found to be child molesters. In some cases, high-ranking Church authorities protected pedophile priests by preventing the authorities from discovering evidence. Is the Catholic Church evil?

At first glance, some of the above questions seem quite easy to answer in the affirmative. However, in each case there are "explanations." So let's run them down before making a final judgment.

Query #1: The rap industry's standard justification for violent, antisocial lyrics is that the message is real and the performers and distributors are just telling the truth about a gritty segment of American society. This is the mantra of those making a killing (sorry) by selling base entertainment to children and young adults (the primary market).

The problem with this rationalization is the exposition of the subject. For example, if you saw the movie *American Gangster,* you got a very real view of the drug-dealing industry. But the main character, a heroin merchant played by Denzel Washington, was not glorified. He was cool in the beginning of the movie, but that persona blew up and the evil of his life was vividly portrayed. Just in case some dimwits didn't get it, Denzel finally wound up being totally humiliated when his elderly mother slapped his face. Lesson: Responsible portrayals of the dark side of American life are possible and can also be profitable, as *American Gangster* proved.

But that lesson will not be heeded by the rap and hip-hop industry. It's too hard and goes against "street cred." The myth that violence and criminality are cool is an essential part of the packaging and marketing of the often vile hip-hop product. Honest people cannot possibly deny the dangerous influence this industry has on some vulnerable children. That's why I believe the people behind this industry are committing evil acts in order to make money, and their rationalizations about "art" and "social commentary" are as ludicrous as the clown prince of rap himself, a guy who calls himself Ludacris. Well, at least he got that right.

Query #2: The torture-film people don't have a tortuous explanation for their abysmal behavior; they have a simple one: it's only a movie. What's the big deal? Everybody knows motion pictures are fiction; there's nothing real about the pain and suffering gleefully inflicted on-screen.

Except it's sickening.

If you think about it, the torture industry is very easy to explain. Simply put, it makes a product for sadistic people to enjoy. The more suffering on-screen, the better. Let's get a close-up of that arm being amputated and that eyeball being gouged out. Again, it's all about money. Why else would anyone spend time and resources filming ways to hurt people? Where is the good in that?

The answer, of course, is that there is no good in that. Only evil. Simply put, anyone who delights in portraying or watching human suffering is sick. Got it?

Query #3: The vast majority of child abusers are evil, no doubt. Anyone who physically or mentally hurts a child is committing an evil act, and those who do it on a regular basis are in a league with murderers and rapists.

But wait, what about intoxicated adults who hurt kids while under the influence? The trend these days is to define alcoholism and drug dependency as a disease, something that the substance abuser has little control over. In fact, there are doctors who will tell you that chemical addicts have a brain dysfunction that drives them to seek an intoxicated state. So if they can't help themselves, how can we call their activities evil? And if, while stoned, they hurt a child or anyone else, it isn't really their fault; they have a disease they can't control!

Good grief!

Again, this goes back to free will and my belief that we all *choose* between doing good or committing evil. Yes, sometimes a person can get caught up in a situation where he or she commits a dreadful act, like hurting a child, as a result of making a very poor decision, such as failing to control a temper. Okay. But to do it more than once is inexcusable.

By the way, you don't catch an addiction like you catch a cold. You acquire it. You *choose* to put the bottle or pipe to your lips, the needle to your arm. But you could choose otherwise, as millions of former addicts have demonstrated. Despite legions of excuse makers who enable evil, compulsive behavior can be defeated if the will is present to do so.

Summing up, all child abuse is evil, and most abusers are bad people. We don't have to get more complicated than that. Occasionally, child abuse can be defined as a terrible onetime act and not a consistent pattern of calculated evil. But repeat offenders should get no quarter, and they can expect their own lives to degenerate into living hells. Not to mention the real hell that will surely come later.

Query #4: Here's the key question: how can terrorism exist if rational human beings know that murdering innocent women and children is the most cowardly act on earth? The answer is complicated, but, in the end, it comes down to untreatable mental illness. Osama bin Laden and his crew are not discernibly different from Hitler, Mao, or Stalin. Shrinks define them as sociopaths, but that is a clinical term for the hospital or classroom. In the everyday world, these men are simply evil and must be isolated or killed so that innocent people can be protected from their treachery.

But, Lord, there are so many of these barbarians. There are millions of human beings who have killed or will kill people because they believe some god or the führer or whoever has ordered that. If you still resist the idea of active evil in the world today, just picture the nineteen 9/11 hijackers killing three thousand people for absolutely no reason. Time after time, history has shown us that this kind of murderous conduct is part of the human condition. But still, some on this earth refuse to believe that evil exists and that terrorism is the epitome of it. Getting people to understand that truth is central to the struggle of our times.

Bottom line: terrorist killers and those who support them are evil. Period.

Query #5: Imagine a trusted priest sexually molesting your child. It happens all the time. And sometimes, after he is discovered, the priest is actually protected by his superiors in the Church. So how evil is that?

But, again, there's an excuse. The priest needs "treatment." He has a disease, a mental compulsion he cannot control. He is sorry. Doesn't everybody deserve forgiveness? That is a cornerstone of Judeo-Christian philosophy, is it not?

That's how some leaders in the Catholic Church framed the most devastating scandal American Catholicism has ever seen.

Of course, most of that argument is nonsense. The molesting priest committed a heinous crime and should have been turned over to the authorities immediately for punishment. Jesus was clear about that: render unto Caesar. Let God forgive the sinner, but justice should be meted out on earth. If not, how would the kids be protected in the here and now?

Catholic leaders like Cardinal Law in Boston and Cardinal Mahony in Los Angeles made a calculated decision to try to conceal these wretched criminals and hush up their crimes. Those supporting the cardinals say they did this to protect the Church from a devastating public scandal. In other words, in pursuit of the "greater good" for their religion, Law and Mahony somewhat understandably hid the evil.

Nonsense. Another bogus rationalization.

The cardinals certainly know that molesting a child is an evil act that must be harshly punished. Treatment can come later. Way later. But, I believe, many big shots in the American Catholic Church simply were looking out for themselves. Any scandal in their dioceses would reflect poorly on them in Rome. The Pope would be angry.

I could be wrong about that, but I'm not wrong about this: much evil is done in the name of God by people claiming to serve the deity. This is the ultimate betrayal, the top of the evil pyramid. God does not sanction murder, child abuse, or any other kind of destructive behavior. The priest pedophilia scandal was evil. No question.

By the way, a number of Catholics actually abandoned their faith over the scandal, a perplexing move that we'll deal with in the next chapter. But to cap this chapter, I have another short story.

Back in 1962, there were sixty kids in my eighth-grade class, which was taught by an elderly nun named Sister Mary Martin. We know that she was a perceptive woman because she wrote this comment on the back of my report card: "Socializes quite freely yet resents correction!"

Pithy and accurate.

Upon reading that, my father was his usual blunt self: "What the hell does that mean?"

"I'm popular," I said.

"Get less popular," he said.

"Okay."

Anyway, there was a girl in the class named Norma. She had been transferred into our group in seventh grade because she was slow academically. In fact, Norma was fifteen, two years older than the rest of the class. Although she was well developed physically, mentally who could tell? Norma just sat there day after day and stared.

Many of the kids were brutal toward Norma, teasing her mercilessly. I couldn't be bothered with tormenting her, because I had my sights set on doing that to the nuns. But I didn't stick up for Norma,

"There is in reality but one subject: God, man, and nature in their relation to one another, a relation wherein good and evil, truth and beauty, life and death, history and futurity meet in one."—Rev. A. Gratry.

To the PARENT or GUARDIAN:

The School aims to stimulate the God-given creative powers of the child. Achievement should be judged in relation to the student's own abilities, not on the basis of unfair comparison with others. Superior work is expected of the bright; effort is demanded of all.

Special attention should be given to progress in reading since this skill influences all learning. Marks result from class work as well as Quarterly Examinations.

SR. M. THOMASINE ———— PRINCIPAL

Teacher's remarks (if any)

1st Quarter:

2nd Quarter:

3rd Quarter: *Socializes quite freely, yet resents correction!*

4th Quarter:

Signature of Parent or Guardian

1st Quarter: *William J. O'Reilly*

2nd Quarter: *William J. O'Reilly*

3rd Quarter: *William J. O'Reilly*

4th Quarter:

either. I probably even encouraged the cruel behavior by laughing along with it.

A couple of years later, in high school, I got bullied a bit and remembered Norma's ordeal. Karma. I took the bullies on, as is my style, but the whole thing was painful, even though it was nothing compared to what Norma endured. To this day, I have never forgotten Norma and her ordeal. The teasing was unrelenting. It was evil.

The thing is, the kids in my class were good kids. Not one of them had a malevolent heart. I spent eight years with those people, and I know them. A few years ago, I set up a St. Brigid's reunion, and eighty percent of my classmates showed up. And they are still good people, solid citizens.

But what we all did to Norma was wrong.

The point is that good people do bad things all the time. Every person on this earth has a capacity for evil. Most people fight against that impulse, but everybody has it.

As a leader in that St. Brigid's class and a rather large, tough kid, I could have stopped the daily garbage directed at Norma. I should have stopped it. And when a similar thing happened to me, I vowed I would never again allow bullying in my presence. Years later, as a high school teacher, I made life hell for the campus bullies. Even more years later, in the media, I go after child abusers with a vengeance. Norma taught me a lesson I have never forgotten.

You either fight active evil or you accept it. Doing nothing is acceptance. There is no in-between.

CHAPTER 5

RELIGION

Let the sun shine in,
Face it with a grin.
'Cause smilers never lose,
And frowners never win.

—ST. BRIGID'S SCHOOL SONG

O n my eleventh birthday, September 10, 1960, Hurricane
Donna smashed into Fort Myers, Florida, and then roared
up the East Coast, pounding the New York City area two days later.
Donna still holds the record for the longest-running killer hurricane.
Over a nine-day period, fifty Americans died. Unfortunately, the
eye of the storm, an incredible one hundred miles wide, passed directly over Long Island, where I lived.

I vividly remember that day because my mother actually made
me leave the house in the midst of winds and rains lashing the
neighborhood. And what was the emergency that forced me out into
the fierce storm? Well, it wasn't complicated: I had to serve the
eight a.m. Mass, and no act of God was going to interfere with that
duty, if my mom had anything to say about it. So she fired up the

Nash Rambler and off we went to St. Brigid's Church, alarming gusts of wind rocking the boxy red car the entire way. (An interesting side note: the Rambler was made by the American Motors Corporation, which was run by George Romney, Mitt's father.)

Winifred Angela O'Reilly, Ann to her friends, was a *very* devoted Catholic, and that was that. Unlike my father, who set the rules and the tone in the house, my mother did not ask much. She was very kind and nice. She made Laura Bush look like a Hell's Angel.

One of the few things my mother ever requested of me—besides demanding that I not tie up my little sister again—was to be an altar boy. She *really* wanted that. And even though memorizing a bunch of Latin prayers and getting up at six in the morning to kneel on a cold marble altar was not my idea of a great time, I did what my mother wanted with a minimal amount of whining. You see, there is *some* good in the bold, fresh guy.

Anyway, we made it to the stone church, I put on my cassock and surplice that is the altar-boy uniform, and the Mass began. I remember Hurricane Donna roaring outside the church as I answered Father Ellard's prayer: *"Mea culpa, mea culpa, mea maxima culpa."* ("Through my fault, through my fault, through my most grievous fault.")

Those words are part of the Confiteor, a prayer expressing responsibility and sorrow for sins. Even though I had no idea what most of the Latin words actually meant, that prayer is fairly obvious, and I got through it perfectly.

That was important, because some of the priests would scold you if you screwed up the ancient language. Father Brodeur was the worst. Amazingly cranky, this priest would yell at you if you messed up *ad Deum* or something. I mean, come on, Father, I'm eleven. Cicero and Pliny the Elder aren't exactly in my wheelhouse. It's seven in the morning and you're obsessed with the pronunciation of *Oremus*? Jesus would have let it go.

And Father Ellard would have ignored it as well, because, unlike some of his compatriots, he was a good guy. He was also very old and, I suspect, couldn't hear very well. So he never admonished the altar boys and finished saying Mass in record time. Some days, Father Ellard could have you breathing fresh air in twenty minutes. He was a great man of God.

We kids also went to his confessional stall in great numbers. Again, it might have been the hearing thing again, because no matter what you told Father Ellard, no matter how horrendous your indiscretions, your penance was three Hail Marys. Charles Manson would have gotten three Hail Marys.

This sanction was excellent, especially given the options. For example, if you confessed your sins to Father Tierney, a nasty little guy, you might wind up in the church basement chained to the wall. But Father Ellard definitely had the right theological attitude for dopey kids: quick Mass and leniency for puerile sinners.

Very early on, I learned to accept the fact that I was an Irish Catholic and that the tradition was valuable. It's interesting. There is no question but that I was a difficult child, a complete nonconformist with very little common sense and a below-average attention span. That is not a good combination.

Yet, somehow, I recognized that Catholicism was basically a good thing, even though some of the people associated with it were loons. Unlike many, I never equated crazy priests and mean nuns with the core tenets of the faith. I just thought they were bad employees. I never took their nuttiness and applied it to Jesus or even to the Pope. To my limited mind, Jesus came off as a pretty good guy. He ran around healing people, was nice to his mom, and even forgave the savages who nailed him to the cross. As the song says: "Jesus is just all right with me."

Not that I was a Jesus freak. Even though I served on the altar, I was the second-biggest sinner ever to attend St. Brigid's School. My classmate Clement was first, as you'll soon see. And please don't misunderstand: our "sins" were minor compared to those of al Qaeda or many television executives. But we did consistently disobey the rules, mock those in authority, and brazenly challenge the accepted wisdom.

Well, okay. You're right. My behavior back then was not much different from what it is today.

Sin City

And now, let me introduce Clement, who should be in the Fresh Kid Hall of Fame. Stocky, with black hair and pale white skin, the boy had no fear. I, at least, feared my father, but Clem was ultradaring; he'd pretty much do anything.

For example, our fifth-grade teacher, Sister Mary Carolyn, became obsessed with reforming Clement. Throughout the school year, the nun used a variety of psychological techniques in an ongoing attempt to shape him up. Of course, her efforts were futile. Clement was a confirmed outlaw.

One day, Sister Carolyn tried the proven counterinsurgency strategy of trying to get the dissenter to buy into the system by giving him authority. Believing Clem might turn his wayward conduct around if granted some responsibility, the nun decided to award him a daily task. This idea was completely insane, but there was no Dr. Phil back then to intervene.

And so the clueless nun put Clement in charge of opening and closing the huge windows that lined the east side of the classroom. Reaching the tops of the windows required using a long, lancelike metal pole, which would hook onto latches so the windows could be pulled down. Thus, a long, heavy, warlike item was placed in his hands? My pal Clem was salivating.

Soon after becoming the pole guy, Clement made his move. With Sister Carolyn facing the blackboard, her back to the class, Clement promptly whacked Kenny H. with the metal pike. Kenny howled, causing the good sister to whirl around in great alarm. He quickly fingered Clement, who was actually still holding the semilethal weapon. But, stunningly, Clement denied the charge. The entire class had witnessed the misdemeanor, but nobody gave Clement up. We all sat there mute when Sister Carolyn asked for confirmation. Kenny was going nuts, but the class stayed silent.

I can still remember Clement wailing in his New York accent: "I didn't do it, Sista; everybody's always blaming me."

Now, the nun might have been naive, but she wasn't stupid. Furious, she ran down the aisle, grabbed the pike, and fired Clement from his job. He was also given demerits or something, which mattered not in the least to Clem, who relished demerits the way most kids savor ice cream.

By my reckoning, Clement committed at least three sins that day: assault, lying, and gloating about lying afterward. While visions of hellfire often danced in the heads of many Catholic schoolkids, Clem seemed to have no fear of eternal damnation. On some level, you have to admire that.

And speaking of sin, fortunately there was an antidote. On the first Friday of every month, the entire St. Brigid's student body was force-marched into the church to go to confession, which is one of the seven Catholic sacraments. There was no getting out of it unless you could convince your mom that you were sick and she let you stay home. And on confession day, every kid in my class, all sixty of them, knew you never got behind Clem in the line. Ever.

That's because whatever Clement was telling the priest usually teed him off so much that he'd take it out on the next few penitents. One time Clement foolishly entered Father Tierney's stall, and moments later the priest actually yelled, "You did *what*?" . . . his voice echoing throughout the church. Some of the girls actually trembled.

At lunchtime, we all pleaded with Clement to tell us what he told

Father Tierney. We even offered him money. But Clem just smiled and walked away. I hate using the word *cool,* but there's no way around it: Clement was a very cool guy.

As you can see, my take on Catholicism is sprinkled with humor and affection. Today, there are more than 60 million American Catholics, and each one has a unique relationship with the religion. That's because it is complicated and emotional. Other kids were very intense, even intimidated by Catholic teaching, but not the bold, fresh guy. I embraced the good stuff—like the outstanding Christmas rituals and the fun of St. Patrick's Day—and took the bad stuff—like hell—in stride.

For some, the bad stuff included Catholic school, which was not exactly a hayride. There have been so many things written about Catholic education that clichés abound. So let me set the record straight from one survivor's viewpoint.

In the 1950s and '60s, "old-school" rules still applied. That meant corporal punishment was acceptable, a strict regimen of spelling, writing, and long division was an everyday occurrence, and Jesus was a constant topic of conversation.

Years later, I look back and appreciate most of that. The slapping was extreme, but the academic discipline and emphasis on loving your neighbor as yourself set me apart from many of my public-school friends. I still played with them every day after school, but as I got older, I noticed a difference in the way we looked at life. Temptations like drugs, alcohol, and violent behavior were major deals for me. I was trained (brainwashed?) to resist them. Some of my secular friends were not.

Also, the constant teaching about Jesus resulted in an indelible role model for many Catholic schoolkids, myself included. There's a reason that the cross is the symbol of Christianity. It is a powerful statement: that a good man suffered for me, that a just God was looking out for me, and if I lived a good life, I would be rewarded after death. Those beliefs, sincerely held, can get a human being through many hard times.

Fortunately, most Americans agree with my analysis. According to a Pew Research study, more than ninety percent of those living in the USA believe in God, eighty-one percent describe themselves as Christian, and eighty-five percent say their religion is an important part of their lives.

I believe that a concentration of believers has made America a strong, noble country. As I got older and learned more about history, I saw how the Founding Fathers used Judeo-Christian philosophy to forge the Constitution, perhaps the most perspicacious political document ever designed. I also understood how a strong belief in good over evil enabled the USA to defeat godless enemies like Nazi Germany, the Japanese emperor (who was regarded as a god), and the Soviet Union. Yes, there have been bad things done under the banner of religion in America. But, on balance, the United States has benefited greatly by the mass belief Americans hold in a just, compassionate God.

As I wrote in *Culture Warrior,* I never had a problem believing in a higher power because of nature. It works. There's never a "miscommunication." Everything man gets involved with is fraught with uncertainty. But every morning the sun comes up.

Some think an asteroid or something caused the natural order. Wow. Talk about blind faith!

So combining a good guy like Jesus with a higher power that created a stunningly efficient natural universe was relatively easy for a simple guy like me. There was no major downside to being Catholic, except, of course, the inconvenience of actually obeying the rules. There's always a catch.

There is no doubt that many people who attended Catholic school see things differently than I do. Some say the experience damaged them. And I respect their dissent, as every school situation is unique.

I also respect every other religion that promotes goodwill toward all people. In my view of life, spirituality is a very positive thing, and faith is a personal matter that should be accepted as such. If someone tells me that I am going to hell because I don't believe as they do, I simply put three letters next to their name: N-U-T.

One of the blessings that I was given (not by an asteroid) is the ability to think for myself. So all the while I was going through St. Brigid's School, I was doing that. I absorbed the lessons, challenged them often, and ultimately decided that the faith I was born into was the one I would die with. My call, and I'm glad I made it.

Along the way there were certainly times when I could have chucked the Catholic way of life. Some of my friends did. But I hung in there despite some tension between the Church establishment and me. As mentioned, many of my teachers marked me as a very bad influence, a troubled and wayward youth. I know you may find that hard to believe.

In the fourth grade, for example, our teacher, Aimee Martin, a Catholic layperson, put me in the "dumb row," where I most assuredly belonged. Located closest to the windows, this row of desks was reserved for students who were not exactly lighting it up academically, if you know what I mean. Immediately, I was smart enough to figure out how foolish it was to locate the dumb row by the windows. Question: What do dumb kids often like to do during class? Why, look out the window, of course. Pretty dumb of you, Mrs. Martin, I must say.

Unlike some in the dumb row, I had no self-esteem issues about being there. In fact, it was fun. Clement was a dumb-row denizen, and a couple of my other friends were too. So, instead of being ashamed, I pulled a Tom Sawyer and convinced the class that the hippest kids inhabited the dumb row. My spin went like this: Mrs. Martin was clueless (unanimous agreement), and Clement was the coolest guy in town. Do the math (tough for dumb rowers): the window row was the place to be.

Before long, Mrs. Martin got wind that the dumb-row assignation was no longer a humiliation but had somehow evolved into a status symbol. Furious, she upped the ante, hoping to further humiliate us by constantly berating the row. However, the more she ranted, the more prestigious the row became. It was anarchy in the finest sense.

Clement and I celebrated this unlikely success by upping the ante ourselves and openly mocking Mrs. Martin. Looking back, that was wrong, probably a venial sin. But the teacher did deserve some of the grief we gave her, no question. More important, the fourth grade was a crucial turning point in all our lives: from that time on it was guerrilla warfare between my classmates and our teachers all the way through to the eighth grade. We had thousands of laughs. The insurrection was permanent; nothing the teachers could do stemmed the tide. No child was left behind; we were united: us against them, no wavering.

Even under the feared rule of Sister Thomas.

The Hairy Eyeball

If Ivan the Terrible had a sister, she would have been Sister Mary Thomas, a nun whose great regret in life was that she missed the Inquisition. The year was 1961, the month September. The Berlin Wall had just been erected, John Kennedy was in the White House, Mister Ed, a talking horse, was huge on TV, and Ray Charles was advising Jack to hit the road.

None of that, however, mattered in the least to our seventh-grade class sitting before a young nun with an attitude. We were just trying to survive. To call Sister Thomas "unusual" is like calling Michael Moore a liberal. It doesn't even come close.

As I write these words, I am staring at my seventh-grade class

Bill O'Reilly

Sister Mary Thomas's reign of terror.
That's Clem, twelfth from the left, two guys away from Sister.

photo. The girls are all sitting at their desks, Laura D. and Kathy M. anchoring the front row. The guys are standing in the back, lined up according to height. I am the second-tallest, positioned between Greg (the aforementioned Bear) and Kenny H. of pole-bashing fame.

In the midst of the boys stands Sister Thomas, her black-and-white habit (the name for the nun uniform) shrouding all but her pale white face. Wearing black-rimmed glasses and a very slight smile, the nun looks to be about thirty years old. Most of my classmates are smiling, but out of fear, not mirth. Everybody knew that Sister Thomas would see the class picture, and anybody defiling it would be subject to major unpleasantness.

Unlike most teachers at St. Brigid's School, who toed the Catholic line but were somewhat gentle in doing so, Sister Thomas was a fanatic, a hellfire advocate who brooked no nonsense. Every morning she would order the class to take out *The Baltimore Catechism* (which listed Catholic teaching) and chant the following: "A mortal sin is a deadly sin. A venial sin is a lesser sin."

She would then define mortal and venial sins, putting a unique spin on the abominations:

Mortal:
- Slow dancing with chests touching
- Anything involving the tongue except talking and eating
- Thinking about the above (except talking and eating)
- Not going to Sunday Mass
- Not telling every single sin to the priest in confession
- Not praying to the Virgin Mary for forgiveness of sins
- Not doing everything the Church and your parents tell you to do
- Not being "sincere" in your penance

Venial:
- Hitting your siblings

As you can see, mortal sins dominated, and drastic punishment, eternal damnation, was the price. Sister Thomas often told the touching story of two "youngsters" who had committed some kind of impurity. Tragically, before they could reach the confessional, they were killed in a car wreck. Sometimes a train demolished the car. Other times the car simply got wrecked with no explanation. Incredibly, Sister Thomas had tapped into popular culture with this story line. A pop song called "Teen Angel" had become a big hit in February of 1960. Some will remember the song's refrain, sung by a teenage boy holding the hand of his dead girlfriend, who had just been annihilated by a train:

Teen angel, can you hear me?
Teen angel, can you see me?
Are you somewhere up above?
And am I still your own true love?

Good grief! The nun even had *American Bandstand* helping her.

Even at age twelve, a lot of the kids were deeply affected by Sister Thomas's harsh vision of life, but not Clement and not the bold, fresh guy. Often, we would discuss the nun at recess, and most of the time the conversation was in the mortal-sin category. The nun tortured us, but we would not let her prevail. Revenge was in the air.

The conflict had been brewing for a while. Even before the 1961–62 school year had started, Sister Thomas knew Clem and Billy O'Reilly. She had heard the stories and she relished the challenge. One time, in the sixth grade, Clem and I were standing together at some school assembly and she walked over.

"I'm looking forward to having you two gentlemen in my class next year."

No more frightening words were ever spoken.

Tragically, Sister Thomas got her wish, and the ensuing nine months were the longest of my life. She had sonar hearing, picking up every whisper. The nun had a long list of infractions, with each bit of bad behavior earning its own specific punishment:

- Talking out of turn—slap on the hand with a ruler.

- Talking back to sister—slap in the face, often hard.

- Being a wise guy in general—note home to parents, which had to be signed and brought back to her (this usually led to domestic punishment, at least for me).

- Sloppy appearance or work—after-school detainment.

- Teasing girls Sister Thomas liked—trip to the principal (Sister Mary Thomasine), likely leading to after-school yard work along with a severe scolding.

The list of sanctions went on and on. Sister Thomas's seventh-grade class wasn't an academic experience; it was a prisoner-of-war camp.

But the absolute worst was her signature face-to-face confrontation. Staring down into your eyes, her eyeballs darted crazily back and forth. We called it the "hairy eyeball," and it was truly eerie. Having that nun in your face was a terrifying experience rivaling a viewing of *Not of This Earth.*

But revenge is a dish best served cold.

Let 'Er Rip

A few times a year, the entire school body would participate in an activity. In the fifth grade, for instance, we all marched down to the Westbury movie theater to see Jennifer Jones in the classic 1943 film *The Song of Bernadette,* for which Ms. Jones won an Academy Award. The thinking here was to use a Hollywood film to reinforce the Catholic faith. Since the movie jaunt got us out of math and English, the outing was fine with me.

Unfortunately, all plans can go awry, and this one proved that beyond a reasonable doubt. The turn-of-the century theater had an extensive balcony from whence water balloons were launched just as the Virgin Mary was appearing to Jennifer. Pandemonium ensued; the sanctity of the occasion was lost.

Clem and I denied any part in the sacrilege. One of us was lying.

In the spring semester of our seventh-grade ordeal, Sister Thomas was given the honor of having her class perform a play for the entire school, parents included. I guess the administration believed that if anyone could control a student performance, it would be the taskmaster nun. But, to quote my mom whenever I asked for something, "We'll see."

That year, 1962, was tremendous for pop music. The Beatles launched their first single in America, "Love Me Do," Chubby Checker was twisting his butt off, and a real teen angel, Shelley Fabares of *The Donna Reed Show,* had a huge hit with a song called "Johnny Angel." The girls in my class loved Shelley; the guys liked a new show called *McHale's Navy.* We were all twisting like insane people. My classmate Marlene named her new dog Chubby.

Against that cultural landscape, Sister Thomas selected *Rip Van Winkle* as the play her seventh-grade class would perform. A classic tale, the Washington Irving short story involved a guy falling asleep for decades, largely because a mean woman was "henpecking" him. Many boys under Sister Thomas's tutelage immediately identified with Rip.

Everyone in the class was assigned a part except Clement and the bold, fresh guy. The reasons were obvious, and Clem and I didn't much care. Until, that is, we learned that while our classmates rehearsed, we'd have to do "busy work." We were ordered to fill out multiple pages in our *Think-and-Do Book*s (real name) and, by the end of the day, turn them in to Sister.

An outrage! While the rest of class played, we had to work? Unthinkable.

So we decided to plead our case. We went to Sister Thomas and politely asked to be included. Unbeknownst to us, this was exactly what the nun wanted. She believed that we would lose face if we whined about the exclusion. So she publicly mocked us, explaining to the kids that we had come hat in hand to her, asking for parts in the play. Rolling her weird eyes, she then put our request to a vote by the class. Should Billy and Clement be included? What say you?

Unanimously, the people spoke: Of course they should be included! How else would chaos be assured?

Clement was given a very—and I mean very—small part as a rock in the Catskill Mountains. Along with several other urchins, he placed his face in a scenery cutout; in unison he and all the "mountain rocks" were supposed to bellow: "POOR RIP AND POOR WOLF."

That dramatic line occurred immediately after Rip Van Winkle drank some kind of potion and dozed off. The mountain rocks were supposed to say the line three times. Wolf, by the way, was Rip's dog. He didn't fall asleep, but the mountains felt sorry for him anyway.

After that scene, about ten seconds overall, the Catskill Mountains were never seen onstage again. Sister Thomas was taking no chances.

Likewise, I was given a bit part. I was a Dutchman. Along with five other guys, I was to pretend to roll a bowling ball and say: "THE FLAGON, THE WICKED FLAGON!"

The "wicked flagon" was a large cup from which poor Rip had sipped. Apparently, that cup was wicked. Perhaps it had French-kissed another cup.

Anyway, it took me days, but I learned my line, and Clement had his dialogue down as well.

As performance day approached, Sister Thomas was feeling mighty good about things. She was actually jaunty, putting the finishing touches on everything Rip Van Winkle. Her two class pets had the lead roles—Richie as Rip and Diane as Dame Van Winkle—and all was right with the world.

Then it happened, as fate dictated. Two days before airtime, Clement approached me on the playground.

"Billy, we have to do something."

I didn't like the sound of that at all, but he continued.

"All the eighth graders will be watching, and I said we'd do something."

"We, Clem? We? Are you insane? So what if the eighth graders are watching? So's every nun and priest in the parish, plus my mother and your mother."

"Yeah, it'll be great."

"What'll be great?"

"When we wreck the play."

For the first time, I saw Clement clearly, even though I'd known him since he was five years old. He was *truly* demented. By the seventh grade, Clem was already shaving a couple of times a week, and his outlook on life was far beyond that of the average twelve-year-old. On that spring day more than forty-five years ago, I stared hard at my pal, and the gleam in his eye said it all: *I don't care.*

"Clem, I don't want to die. I can't wreck the play."

To this day, I can still remember the sadness that crossed Clement's face. His compadre was chicken, his pal a wuss. He silently shook his head and walked away.

For a second, I felt terrible. Then I regained what little sense I had. To sabotage Sister Thomas's play was a truly desperate act. There would be no escaping the inevitable retribution certain to follow. Why didn't we just lie down on the Northern State Parkway?

To my discredit, I did not try to talk Clement out of his insanity, perhaps because a large part of me wanted to see Sister Thomas humiliated. But I knew Clem was going to get hurt; there was no doubt.

Soon the day arrived and the auditorium was packed. From backstage, we peered out at the assemblage: parents, teachers, students, even the parish pastor, Father Code. This was big.

Somewhere in the crowd sat my mother. No way my father was going to sit through *Rip Van Winkle* unless he had a number of flagons filled with refreshment, and that was not happening. But Mom was actually looking forward to seeing her son in his dopey Dutchman outfit. Moms are amazing.

No question but that Sister Thomas thought she was Steven Spielberg. She ran from one kid to the next, making sure the costumes were fitted correctly and nobody was throwing up. We were all nervous—everybody, that is, except Clement. He sat serenely backstage, but I knew that look.

Wayne was really scared. Dressed in a shabby canine outfit, he was playing Rip's dog, Wolf, and had to crawl around following the leading man, Richie. Even though Wayne had no lines, he was petrified.

Clement noticed Wayne too. And then I noticed Clem noticing Wayne. Uh-oh. I remember thinking that somehow this was not going to turn out well for Wayne.

The curtain rose, and for the first few minutes everything went swell. Sister Thomas sat to the right of the stage, following the script on her clipboard. Most of the kids were stage left. Nobody really wanted to hang close to the notorious nun.

The first sign of trouble came when Rip drank from the flagon and slumped to the ground. Somehow, he landed on Wayne's paws, causing his faithful pet to fall down. Big laughs from the crowd.

Cue the mountain rocks. Remember, they were supposed to say in unison, "Poor Rip and poor Wolf." But one voice bellowed above the rest, completely out of sync.

Does the name Clement mean anything?

While the other rocks wailed, "Poor Wolf!" Clem drowned them out by screaming, "AND RIP IS POOR TOO! HE DOESN'T HAVE MONEY! THAT ISN'T FAIR!"

Massive laugh from the eighth graders.

Sister Thomas's face turned Alabama crimson. Those eyes darted all over the place like some kind of crazy pinball game. As the curtain fell for a scene change, Clement bolted. I later learned he fled to the sanctuary of the boys' bathroom.

I actually prayed to Saint Michael the Archangel for Clem. I hoped that prank was it, that he had established his eighth-grade cred and the play would conclude without further chaos. My scene came next, but

I don't remember it. My mother says I did fine and she could hear me call the flagon "wicked." But it's all a blur to me.

However, the play's climax remains crystal clear in my mind. I can actually see it in slow motion. After Rip comes back from his snooze and all is well in the town, the main characters gather for a bow. But Wayne is not onstage. Instead, Clement is inside the dog costume and is furiously biting Richie on the leg. Rich frantically tries to get away, but Clem hangs on, actually sinking his teeth into the poor kid. There's yelling, scuffling, pandemonium.

Curtain.

Clement was suspended for two weeks, which was pretty much the rest of the term. There was talk of expulsion, but his mother, a daily Mass communicant, threw herself on the mercy of the court. Clem was allowed to return for a hilarious eighth-grade ride, but I'll save that for another book.

After the play debacle, Sister Thomas said very little to the class. With only a couple of weeks left in the school year, she gave us our exams and prayed many, many rosaries. Nobody got whacked with the ruler during those final days, even though we constantly discussed a forbidden topic: the hysteria of the performance.

Wayne told me that Clement simply took him out. Wayne was a little guy, and Clem was strong, so the costume hijack was accomplished in seconds. I asked Wayne if Clem had said anything. Wayne said yeah: "Gimme the dog suit."

Okay.

Yeah, Yeah, Yeah, I'm Keepin' the Faith

Billy Joel understands the Long Island experience because he lived it, and I'll submit to you that much of what I witnessed as a child remains indelible. I remember nearly everything about St. Brigid's

School. Those were great times, and they solidified my relationship with Catholicism, because everything was tied in together: memorable classmates, coming of age, a charitable philosophy, and a sense that life has a purpose if you live it generously.

I may have been in the dumb row, but, eventually, I figured it all out.

After graduation the following year, my father forced me to go to a strict Catholic high school, Chaminade, where my religious education continued. He made the right call. Even though I wanted to go to the public school with my thug friends, my dad understood that I needed continual structure and discipline. To this day, Chaminade leads the league in that. There is no doubt that twelve years of blending academics with spiritual teaching forged my point of view today.

As I've written earlier in chapter three, my arrival at Marist College in the fall of 1967 coincided with a growing secularization of that traditionally Catholic institution. But even as the liberated late sixties blew across campus, I still went to church. On some Sunday mornings, there were about five students staring at the chaplain, a kindly man named Father Leo Gallant. I continued going to Mass because I actually liked the spiritual time-out. Leaving the chaotic college world for a while, I enjoyed getting into another dimension, with apologies to Rod Serling. Mass time allowed me to think and figure out right from wrong. In those years, believe me, that wasn't all that easy.

To this day, I still go to Sunday Mass. Often, it's boring. Many times the priest goes on far too long about the mustard seed. Hey, Father, those of us showing up on Sunday have got that down, okay? Fallow ground is not good. Let's advance the discussion, can we?

In helping me to determine right from wrong, good from evil, and trying to correct injustice, my Catholic faith is invaluable. In public and on TV and radio, I usually keep my religion to myself, because I have a secular job: I'm a journalist, not an evangelist. But if somebody brings up the subject, I tell him or her what I just told you.

Religion has been a very positive thing in my life. Without it, I would never have been motivated to expose bad guys and celebrate heroism. Most media people are self-interested and cautious. But I see my job as much more than a big paycheck and a good table at the bistro du jour. I am on a mission, and it all started in the first grade.

Much later in life, after I had traveled the world as a reporter and witnessed awful things, the final piece of the Catholic puzzle fell into place. Like many people, I often wondered how a just God—that is, the Trinity: Jesus, his Father, and the Holy Spirit—could allow so much pain in the universe. A higher power, the Creator, could certainly stop the madness.

The answer to that vexing question lies in the concept of free will. Christianity teaches that free will defines a human being, separates us from the animals. Human beings have the power to choose which actions to take. Lions do not have that ability; they act on instinct.

Thus, the world of man is a constant struggle between good and evil. And what we choose defines us. The essence of Christianity and most other theologies is embracing good and rejecting evil. If there were no evil present in the world, then there could be no choice. That's why bad stuff has been on display from the beginning of time.

The endgame, of course, is to earn God's reward in the afterlife by rejecting evil. And in Catholicism and other Christian religions, the actions of Jesus demonstrate how to do that.

It all makes perfect sense to me. The Christian ethic defines the decisions I make, both personal and professional. But Sister Thomas was right about one thing: I could be a lot better at this.

Finally, my pal Clement died young. I kept up with him through college and he remained a vibrant spirit. But he always had health problems, and, eventually, they caught up with him. I believe he's in heaven. Jesus could never pass on those laughs.

CHAPTER

SAVING THE WORLD

Don't know much about history,
Don't know much biology.

—SAM COOKE, "WONDERFUL WORLD"

od does have a sense of humor, no question. After watching me terrorize teachers for years, the Almighty dropped a teaching job right into my lap. And you say you don't believe.

The year was 1971, the month September, and every weekday morning at exactly six thirty a.m., Rod Stewart's voice would blare from my clock radio:

Wake up, Maggie, I think I got something to say to you,
It's late September and I really should be back at school.

Well, I was back at school, all right. Specifically, Monsignor Edward Pace High School located in the shabby, tough Florida town of Opa-locka, just north of Miami. (To this day it consistently scores among the highest rates of violent crime in the USA.) This was not the Villages, if you know what I'm saying.

The job happened because the powers-that-were at Pace had a relationship with Marist College and were looking for cheap labor. That would be me. Along with my trusty college roommate, Joe Rubino, I signed on to teach English for less than five thousand dollars. Beginning of story.

Teaching held a good amount of appeal to me. Back in the Woodstock days, I felt I should do something worthwhile with my life; I wanted to help folks. It never occurred to me to sell stocks or insurance. That would be working for the *man.* While I saw nothing particularly wrong with working for the *man,* I knew my father had not benefited from doing that, and, again, I wanted to help improve society. Really.

Plus, there was the strong appeal of south Florida. Rubino and I had done the spring-break thing our senior year, hunting for Connie Francis on the beaches of Fort Lauderdale. We never did find Connie, but there were many, many Connie wannabes on display. All I'll say is this: after I'd spent three years in Poughkeepsie, New York, the sun, surf, and female denizens of south Florida looked mighty fine indeed. So we packed up our gear and headed south.

The first sign of trouble was our assigned "accommodations." Because we were working for slave wages, the principal at Pace set us up with a low-rent apartment near the school.

"You guys are gonna like this," he told me on the phone. "Convenient to everything, and there's a pool."

By "convenient to everything," I guess the guy meant to the half dozen drug dealers who lived in the complex. If you were after weed or cocaine, these accommodations were, indeed, convenient. The pool was there as advertised, but a rusty refrigerator had taken up residence at the bottom of it. This wasn't exactly *Surfside 6.*

We lasted less than thirty minutes in our new digs.

Checking out of the Horror Apartment Complex, we quickly found alternative housing with fewer active felons on the premises. But, incredibly, the principal was rather put off that we had exited his recommended lodging. His annoyance should have signaled me that we would not be dealing with a rational guy at the school helm, but it went over my head.

Hey, Teach, What's Up

As I write, I am looking at myself in the 1972 edition of *The Torch,* the Pace High School yearbook. There I am, sitting in front of a class, hair covering my ears, pork-chop sideburns, and a firm, steely look. I

was no Sister Thomas, but believe the photo: I brooked no nonsense. If a kid clowned around, he or she was sharply warned. Second time, an appropriate sanction was swiftly delivered to the miscreant.

Early on, I was tested, as most young teachers are. In my case, I was just twenty-one years old when I began teaching, and one of my assigned classes was senior English. That meant most of my students were seventeen and eighteen years old. Do the math.

One day a blond girl called me Bill in front of the class. This was against school rules, since all teachers were to be addressed as Mr., Mrs., or Miss. In my mind, the girl had intentionally misbehaved for two reasons: attention and the thrill of it all.

I had prepared myself for this. Before the school year started, I had mapped out a game plan to handle what was sure to be some challenging behavior. I was the new, young teacher on campus. Even in my callow youth, I knew boundaries would have to be quickly established or chaos would ensue.

Understanding that discipline is useless without respect (I think I got that from the Sidney Poitier movie *To Sir, with Love*), I coolly appraised the young girl who had just used my given name.

"Miss Jones [an alias], why don't you explain to the class why you addressed me by my first name when you know that is a breach of etiquette?" I kept my voice calm but authoritative. The "breach of etiquette" line threw her.

"Uh, I don't know," she replied.

"So let me get this straight. You decide to break school rules, taking time away from the class, and you don't know why? Am I understanding you?"

Panic swept across the girl's face, which was deeply reddening. Every kid in the class was staring at her. What started as an attempt to diminish the inexperienced teacher had somehow gone horribly wrong. She sat there mute.

"Okay, Miss Jones, here's what's going to happen," I said sharply. "You are going to write a five-hundred-word composition explaining your actions here today. This will be due tomorrow. If you behave yourself, I'll keep your work private. If you do not, I will read it to the class. Are we clear?"

"Yes, Mr. O'Reilly."

"Good."

That was it. Word of Miss Jones's smackdown spread throughout the Pace campus like fire ants on spilled maple syrup. After that I had little trouble in the classroom. Every student in the school immediately understood that, when Mr. O. was involved, humiliation might be just one stupid comment away.

You see, I understood something many adults never get: the worst thing you can do to a dopey teenager is embarrass him or her in front of their peers. You can yell and scream at kids all day long and accomplish nothing. But holding students accountable for their actions publicly has a major inhibiting effect. Not too many kids (or adults, for that matter) want to become an object of public derision.

One caveat here: this doesn't work on the psycho kids. However, Catholic schools tend to weed them out pretty fast and send them on their way.

Now, there's no question that I had damaged Miss Jones's self-esteem, and today the "enlightened" educators who are embedded in the American education system would probably chastise me for insensitivity. But listen up: I don't care. In the two years I taught at Pace, my methods were effective with hundreds of students, most of whom actually learned some things. Meanwhile, many of the other teachers at Pace presided over undisciplined classroom environments that wasted time and accomplished little. I actually cared whether my students were learning. That's why I allowed Rod Stewart's raspy voice to disturb my slumber. I believed it was my responsibility to create an atmosphere where kids could learn important things without disruption. If a teacher can't or won't do that, the students get hosed.

I realize that might sound self-righteous, but that's how I saw it. I was getting paid to do a job, and no defiant kid was going to stop me. Period.

Even so, I didn't want to damage any kid. Shortly after her indiscretion, I spoke with Miss Jones privately. She cried, and I felt bad. But I explained that what she did was unacceptable, and if she continued that kind of behavior, her life would be the worse for it. Did she get the message? I'd love to tell you that the incident changed her

"So I told him, 'go to detention'."

How I was remembered in the Pace 1972 yearbook.
Definitely not *To Sir, with Love.*

life and she went on to do great things. But the truth is, I don't know how Miss Jones turned out. She was a strange kid. Something was definitely bothering her, and she wasn't the confiding type, at least not with me. Life isn't Sidney Poitier winning over Lulu and the other British toughies on the big screen. Still, never again did Miss Jones, or any other student, disrupt that senior English class, and by the end of the school year, most of those people scored well on the exam I gave them. And, trust me, the test wasn't easy.

The majority of Pace High students came from working-class homes with parents who sacrificed to pay private-school tuition. Ethnically, it broke down this way: fifty percent Hispanic, forty percent white, ten percent black. Cubans dominated the campus. I liked them from the jump; most were hardworking, respectful, and grateful to America for saving them from Castro.

In fact, I had more trouble with the Pace faculty than I did with the kids. Hard to believe, I know. By now you have probably picked up that I have a small problem with authority except when I am it. Then authority is okay.

Many of the faculty and administrators at Pace were "small picture" people. That is, they were clueless about what the kids were doing and thinking and concentrated on enforcing picayune, largely meaningless rules. For example, some faculty members actually busied themselves measuring the skirts of the girls. Each female student was required to wear a standardized sky-blue-colored uniform. However, some of the young ladies were hiking up hemlines in an apparent attempt to imitate Goldie Hawn. Some teachers used rulers to measure the proper skirt length. It was almost surreal.

Meanwhile, a number of girls left the school in a family way, if you know what I mean. But there was little talk of dealing with that or the substance abuse occurring on campus.

Since most students at Pace had little money, glue was the substance of choice that year. Cretins would enter the bathroom stalls, smear it on rags, and inhale. Glassy-eyed, they'd stagger into the classroom.

I cornered one of the leaders of the "rag brigade," a skinny wise guy, and basically told him that, if he didn't knock it off, I would hunt him down off school property and we'd "discuss" things. Apparently, he got the message, and the cheap-high crowd toned it down. By the way, I *would* have hunted him down.

Of course the principal, a corpulent, middle-aged Catholic brother, and most of the teachers had no idea that glue was in vogue. No, they were too busy measuring the skirts of the girls.

It was tough, but I ignored most of the insane faculty-driven minutiae, because there was nothing I could do about it. The principal and his disciples had their agenda, and it wasn't going to change because some wise-guy New York teacher thought it was nuts. But one time I did listen to the Isley Brothers and decided to "fight the power." By the way, that strategy rarely turns out well.

Do Not Try This at Work

I've told some parts of the following story before, but in a different
context. Here the point is that we in America waste far too much time
endlessly discussing stupid stuff. If something is wrong, fix it. Don't
discuss it to death. As actor Eli Wallach stated in *The Good, the Bad,
and the Ugly,* "When you have to shoot—shoot. Don't talk."

As in many Southern states, high school football is big in Florida.
On late summer and fall Friday evenings, thousands of kids attend
games and do what many kids do in the dark: attempt to misbehave.
There's the usual drinking and smoking and cursing out the opposition, the kind of stuff that's been going on for generations. But at
Pace, as our Spartans took the field in red-and-gold uniforms, there
was another huge problem: hot pants!

The garment.

Even at these night games, the average temperature in Miami that
year was about eighty-eight degrees, with humidity at the suicide
level. I mean, it was brutal. So the kids dressed accordingly. That is,
they wore very little.

The attire situation caused great fear and loathing among the faculty
at Pace, and I saw their point: wearing halters and short-shorts, some
of the girls looked like Carmen Electra. Not exactly the image a Catholic high school wants to project, with all due respect to Ms. Electra.

Because the bold, fresh guy has always been a simple man, my
solution to the problem was exceedingly simple: tell the girls that
halters and hot pants were banned at all school events, and if they
violated the rule they would be punished. If they didn't like it, tough.
Go roller-skating.

Simple, right? Easily done. "But noooooo," as the late John Belushi was fond of saying on *Saturday Night Live.* The hot-pants deal
had to be discussed and debated and parsed at faculty meetings over
and over again. It was insane.

Finally, I reached critical mass. A woman teacher named Isabella (alias) stood up and said, "I want to ask the faculty to tell us what is appropriate attire at a 'Foosball' game."

Immediately, my hand shot up, and my roommate, Joe Rubino, put his head in his hands, something he had practiced quite often.

"Yes, Mr. O'Reilly."

I slowly got to my feet and said, "I believe, Isabella, that appropriate football game attire is a helmet, spiked shoes, padded shoulders and thighs, and tight pants to keep the pads secured."

Silence. Then a few muffled guffaws. The principal shot me a look that would have made Hannibal Lecter envious. Everybody knew I had mocked the faculty meeting. I was off the reservation.

The following day, I addressed the hot-pants issue in all my classes, and my message was sage and pithy. I simply stated that any girl who dressed like a cheap tart was foolish and would lose the respect of boys, especially decent guys. I also told the students that boys routinely mocked girls they thought were "easy" and had done so since guys were invented. No further lecture was necessary and there were no threats. I simply asked if anyone had any questions, and nobody did.

Once again, word whipped around the campus. The hot-pants mania subsided, as few teenage girls want to be mocked by teenage boys.

Another victory for the home team, right? Not so fast. Life is full of unintended consequences, and boy, did I make enemies among the faculty. Not that I cared at the time; I did not. I liked most of my students but thought the faculty, by and large, were simpletons. I was wrong. Looking back, *I* was the narrow-minded person, because my arrogance was based on ignorance. The truth is that most of the teachers at Pace were good people; they were just scared to make waves. They needed the job. Not so different from my father.

During my two years teaching high school, I learned an enormous amount about life, liberty, and the pursuit of happiness. But one lesson stands above all the others: you can't save everyone. You can give people opportunities, you can try to help them, but some will not succeed, for a variety of reasons.

Once in a while, I look back at the Pace yearbook and see the kids who washed out in life. Could I have done something different to help them? Perhaps. But I tried as hard as I knew how and have subsequently learned that some human beings simply cannot be saved. It's just life in the real lane.

This insight has shaped my political beliefs and my policy analysis. As we discussed in chapter two, I am big on self-reliance and not enthusiastic about the nanny state. I strongly believe that, in America, each individual succeeds by understanding obligations and doing what is necessary to fulfill them. The government cannot do it for us, cannot drag us through life's daily challenges making sure we're all okay. Those who promise that are charlatans. To repeat what I wrote earlier, if you rely on big government—you'll pay big.

That separates me from someone like Nancy Pelosi, for example, who fervently believes that a huge federal presence can bring prosperity to disadvantaged people and just about everybody else. Speaker Pelosi fervently wants high taxes, a redistribution of wealth through said taxation, and a general welfare system that provides cradle-to-grave entitlements like they have in Holland.

Maybe the Speaker wants that because she, herself, is a very wealthy woman, raised in extremely comfortable surroundings. Maybe she feels some guilt over having that kind of life when others don't. Liberal guilt has been known to happen.

Anyway, I worked awfully hard at Pace trying to wise kids up and succeeded in many cases. But, obviously, not all. Some kids were so emotionally damaged by the time they got to my class that, no matter how hard I tried, I couldn't motivate them to be responsible. Their plight usually mirrored that of their parents. Most of the slackers had big trouble at home.

That kind of scenario is one of the most vexing problems facing America. The government cannot legislate decent parenting. Any clown can have a child. There are no tests, standards, or guidelines for parents unless they violate the child abuse or neglect laws. Therefore, some children will be so traumatized by their upbringing that they will cause society big problems that we all pay for, sometimes with our lives.

So what does society do?

Again, it all comes back to the free will that I believe we all have. Even though a child has it rough, there will come a time when he or she, like all other human beings, is faced with a clear choice: either become a productive citizen or become a problem. Almost every violent criminal I've ever spoken with had a terrible childhood. But if society, out of some misguided compassion, does not hold them accountable for harming others, then the result is anarchy.

As you know, some well-intentioned liberals disagree, arguing for lenient sentences and "rehabilitation," even for heinous child rapists. But that point of view is both dangerous and unfair to both innocent kids and law-abiding adults. The government's first obligation is to protect its citizens, not empathize with those who would harm them.

One student at Pace High School committed a murder. I knew the kid. He had a terrible facial complexion and was subject to bullying beyond belief. Socially, the boy was almost totally isolated. You can imagine the anger that kid held inside himself. But he killed somebody. That's irreversible. No matter what the personality profile, society cannot allow troubled people to inflict harm on others. Period.

That philosophy was shaped by my teaching experience. I was a disciplinarian, as you've seen, but fair. Any student could appeal his or her punishment; I would listen and, sometimes, adjust the sanction. I did that because I remembered Brother Lawrence.

Back in my own high school days, there was class warfare in the

My Chaminade ID card. The tie is a guaranteed clip-on.

hallways of Chaminade, a high-powered, all-boy Catholic school in Mineola, New York. On one side of the aisle were the working-class guys like me, on the other, the rich kids from affluent neighborhoods like Garden City and Locust Valley.

Among Chaminade's host of strict rules was the requirement that students wear jackets and ties every day. As you are now aware, my father was not exactly Oleg Cassini. My closet held a couple of cheap sports jackets and a few clip-on ties. But many of the rich guys were decked out in cashmere sports jackets and nifty blue blazers from Brooks Brothers. I mean, some Chaminade guys even *talked* about clothes. Nobody in Levittown did that.

Anyway, the rich guys looked swell and the working-class guys looked like Rodney Dangerfield and that was that.

Or not. One day, two Garden City guys, looking for trouble, approached me and pulled off my clip-on tie. Being the intellectual that I am, I immediately punched one guy in the head and slammed the other guy hard against a locker, causing big noise. Showing alarming speed, Brother Lawrence was on me, slamming me against another locker.

"Hey, Brother, those two started it," I wailed.

"No fighting in school, O'Reilly. Three days' detention," the Brother snapped.

"What about them?" I asked, an edge to my voice.

"I'll deal with them," the Brother said. "That doesn't concern you."

Doesn't concern me? Good grief. But that was Chaminade back in 1966. The rich guys got preference. The working-class guys got detention. I did my time but never forgot the incident.

So it was that kind of sensibility that I brought to my own high school classroom. If a kid thought he was getting hosed, I would listen. But BS walked in my sphere of influence, and every kid at Pace knew it.

Looking back, I really didn't have to do much in the discipline area. Once the tone was set, most of my classes went smoothly. In fact, kids were clamoring to get into my courses. At the start of the second semester of my first year, hundreds of juniors and seniors signed up for my Contemporary Problems class, all of them knowing that the workload would be fairly heavy.

However, as I mentioned, there is an opposing point of view, and the discipline I brought to teaching does not sit well with some liberal people. Dr. Wayne Dyer, for example, has sold millions of books advising folks on how to deal with life in a rather "holistic" way. Writing in *The Bottom Line/Personal* magazine, Dyer had this to say about teaching:

> Show faith in (a person's) ability to make right decisions, and
> they will generally make them. . . . Education researchers
> have found that the classrooms of authoritarian teachers tend
> to descend into chaos as soon as the teacher steps outside.
> The classrooms of teachers who trust their students will
> do the right thing and usually continue to run smoothly even
> without the teacher.

Dr. Dyer does not cite any research he uses to make that dubious claim, but clearly the man has never read *Lord of the Flies* or figured out that it is far easier to do your own thing than to do the disciplined thing. Put another way, it's more fun to be bad than good, more pleasurable to relax than work your butt off. Your thoughts, Dr. Dyer?

History clearly demonstrates that without structure and accountability, human beings have a tough time staying on the rails. And children must be taught this over and over again: an effective person must incorporate discipline into his or her life, and a just society must demand responsibility from its citizens. I learned that beyond a reasonable doubt while teaching at Pace High and have passed it on ever since.

One more story, and I'll dedicate it to Dr. Wayne. Pace High was generally a dumpy place. Two-story classroom buildings, very few amenities. But during my time at Pace, a nice new gymnasium was built, and the bishop of Miami was coming to bless it. The kids didn't care about the ritual, but it was a chance to miss some classes, so they were jazzed. In anticipation of the event, an assembly was called to go over what the ceremony would entail.

Hundreds of kids sat in the brand-new stands, completely ignoring the principal, who was trying to impose some kind of order so directions could be given for the blessing. Becoming increasingly frustrated, the principal stepped to the microphone and sternly demanded silence. The noise got even louder, the laughter and mocking almost deafening.

This went on for about three minutes, and then, as with the hot-pants discussion, I ran out of patience. Armed with my trusty clipboard and pen, I stepped onto the gym floor, glared at the chattering throng, and began to write down names. Almost immediately the noise began to diminish. As I scanned the crowd, there were fewer and fewer comedians performing. I continued to stare hard at the students. They shut up.

Then I stepped back and gestured to the principal.

Of course, this completely showed the guy up, and he knew it. But once again the lesson was there for all to see: without consequences, kids will go wild. Dr. Wayne Dyer may not know that, but I do. By the way, I didn't do anything to the kids who were mocking the principal, because I had made my point. But once again, I had alienated the powers-that-be in the process. Can you say *recurring theme*?

The months flew by at Pace, and every day I learned something new about human nature, child development, and America in general. I was the educator, but I was definitely getting an education as well.

Take the debate about more money for schools. Every time I hear some pinhead politician grandstand about that issue, I seethe. In most places there are plenty of school resources, and if there aren't, chances are the local school board is stealing. The feds are spending record amounts on education, and school-directed property taxes in many places are obscene.

I taught in a relatively poor school. The books were there, and to do my job, I didn't need anything else besides a working air conditioner. My third-grade teacher, Sister Lurana, had sixty kids in her class, and every one of them could read, write, and do math by age eight. Give me a break. Teaching is about presentation and accountability; money and resources are secondary. The U.S. public school education system has plenty of cash. What it lacks are competent, courageous administrators and creative teachers. Yes, better salaries might attract better people. But teaching is a calling, not a business.

Teaching in south Florida for those two years remains a highlight of my life. Yeah, money was tight. To get extra funds, I got a second job as a bouncer in the Wreck Bar at the Castaways Hotel on the northern end of Miami Beach. Actually, I didn't do much bouncing. My job was to make sure the house band, Tommy Strand and the Upper Hand, didn't commit any on-premises felonies, as drugs and underage girls were known to make appearances in the saloon. To this day, I know every word to Aretha Franklin's hit "Chain of Fools," thanks to Tommy Strand, who sang it every Saturday night.

Those years were hot in south Florida. The Miami Dolphins made it to the Super Bowl in both '72 and '73 and won it the latter year going 17–0, a record that still stands. And get this: Pace High School was located right next to the Dolphins training facility at St. Thomas University. One day, I brazenly sneaked into a Don Shula press conference and actually asked the coach a stupid question. He looked at me like I had spilled ketchup on his shirt.

But after two enjoyable years at Pace, it was time for a change. The administration and I had had enough of each other, so I hit the road. After being accepted by Boston University to study for a master's degree in broadcast journalism, I left south Florida, my roommate, Joe, and scores of other friends. I had mixed feelings about the move. I enjoyed seeing my students learn and become more sophisticated in their world outlook. But I was restless and wanted a bigger stage than a high school classroom. It was time to go.

But before I left Pace, a student dropped the following note in my mailbox:

Mr. O., although this year was pretty bad for me, there was one thing that made up for it. I was lucky enough to have a teacher who cared enough to not only teach the required subject, but also to teach me about life and awareness of others and myself.

I am grateful for having known you.

As any teacher will tell you, that's what it's all about.

7

STANDING YOUR GROUND

Because I love that dirty water,
Oh, oh, Boston, you're my home.

—THE STANDELLS, "DIRTY WATER"

To walk down Boston's Commonwealth Avenue in the autumn of 1973 was to witness history unfolding. Hippies, college kids, booze heads, townies, and actual working people, blue-collar to the highest white-shoe professions, all intermingled daily. In the midst of this diversity they probably shared only one interest in common, and it was a really big deal: President Richard Nixon, long known as "Tricky Dick," was in huge trouble. He might even go to prison. People talked about little else.

For a year, *Washington Post* investigative reporters Carl Bernstein and Bob Woodward, relatively unknown at the time, had been chasing down leads in the Watergate story. Now, thanks largely to them, Nixon was on the ropes. As you can imagine, all of us journalism students at Boston University's School of Public Communication closely followed every twist and turn. Almost every day there were new and exciting stories:

- October 10, Vice President Spiro Agnew quits. Days later, he's indicted for federal income-tax evasion. He would subsequently plead no contest and be convicted.

- October 20, Nixon orders Attorney General Elliot Richardson to fire Watergate Special Prosecutor Archibald Cox, who was aggressively challenging Nixon's dodges. Richardson refuses. Nixon fires him and his deputy, William Ruckelshaus. Robert Bork takes over and fires Cox. All hell is breaking loose around the country after this so-called Saturday Night Massacre.

- Impeachment talk heats up, and to think, just a year earlier Nixon had defeated South Dakota Senator George McGovern in a national landslide. Now his presidency was a shambles. He would resign the following August.

There simply was no better time to be studying journalism in America. I really lucked out. The divisive Vietnam War and the ensuing protests had dramatically changed the country, leading to the Age of Aquarius, where social liberalism blossomed. For example, in 1973 the Supreme Court by a vote of 7–2 affirmed *Roe v. Wade* as the law of the land; for the first time abortion was legal all across the USA. That never would have happened had the country not moved to the left so quickly.

But while the fetus could now be destroyed in the womb, convicted killers had been granted a reprieve, as the Supremes, a year earlier, had ruled the death penalty unconstitutional. The case, *Furman v. Georgia,* was a closely decided 5–4 vote. And as America continued its liberal march, there I was, your budding bold, fresh correspondent, right smack-dab in the middle of it.

But, as they say, let the peace/love buyer beware.

As the "power to the people" brigades reached the height of their influence, self-indulgence and arrogance were bringing many flower children crashing down. Crazy nonsense was all over the place. Violent Black Panthers were celebrated as good guys, while brave U.S. service people fighting for their country were labeled villains. Some awful things were "going down," as Buffalo Springfield sang. For me, the Beatles best summed up the hazy Age of Aquarius atmosphere:

Picture yourself in a boat on a river,
with tangerine trees and marmalade skies.

That would be from "Lucy in the Sky with Diamonds," the song I mentioned in chapter one. Unfortunately, LSD and other drugs were everywhere at BU. Getting stoned was routine. Everybody was doing it. Everybody, that is, but me.

Continuing my antidrug posture, I adopted the same mode of behavior I had at Marist: total abstention from substances. By now, I actually hated drugs, because a couple of my Levittown friends had become hard-core addicts, and I witnessed their degeneration up close and personal. I saw them break the hearts of their mothers. I saw them steal from their fathers and friends. I witnessed their complete debasement and ultimately watched as they destroyed themselves. There was nothing I could do. One died in his thirties; the other went to prison.

Drinking, too—I couldn't stand it. At a high school party, I watched as inebriated kids vomited all over my friend's house. Myles's parents had gone to Florida and foolishly left the eighteen-year-old in charge. Those bombed kids caused thousands of dollars of damage to the place and didn't care a whit. Why? Because they were drunk out of their minds, that's why.

As I've said before, I have never been intoxicated or taken any illegal drug, including marijuana. Now, I know some people think this is weird, but I am proud of it. I made a decision: I did not want to be under the influence of anything other than my own dubious personality. Ever.

So I stood my ground at Boston University and lost some social opportunities because of my antidrug position. So be it. I still had a great time, and I *remember* all of it. And I never hurt anyone or destroyed anything while under the influence. I never vomited in the bushes or drove drunk. Good for me.

Still, I was often alone that year. While strobe lights streaked and bongs stoked up, I went to the movies. *American Graffiti* was my favorite. Where were you in 1962? Well, I was attending St. Brigid's School, learning it wasn't all about me; that's where I was.

Truth be told, I liked my country better pre-Vietnam. It was more fun. The Aquarius deal was too confusing. I mean, John Lennon thought he was a walrus. What was that all about? Grace Slick wanted us to feed our heads. Great. But what happens when you overdose, Grace? Do you feel bad because you encouraged drug use? And Jim Morrison wanted to light our fires; remember that great song? Morrison wound up dead in a bathtub at age twenty-seven.

Where was Lesley Gore when I needed her?

Looking back, I remember being home from school in the summer of '73 and having a very pretty girl from Huntington, Long Island, invite me to a party. As soon as we arrived, a giant cloud of pot smoke hit us right between the eyes.

"Far out," she said.

"Let's get out," I answered.

One of us departed.

Confronting Hatred

Upon reflection, I count my stand against the temptations of the time as another major turning point in my life. Instead of chasing Jefferson Airplane's "White Rabbit," I concentrated on pursuing a career. While some other BU students devolved into being dazed and confused on a daily basis, I was focused and determined. I was going to be the next Woodward or Bernstein, whichever one was better-looking.

By the way, as with my religious beliefs, I did not openly criticize those who took up the stoned life unless they were very close to me. Then I'd try to persuade them back to sobriety. And to this day, I don't lecture people about their personal behavior unless it harms another person. I have too much on my karmic rap sheet to be throwing stones at anyone else. Besides, people like Hunter S. Thompson made a good living in journalism actually using chemicals as a prop. But, as you may know, Thompson eventually killed himself, so maybe he's not a great example.

Anyway, as 1974 unfolded, the dramatic action continued. President Ford eventually pardoned Nixon, probably dooming his own reelection chances. Ford also pardoned the Vietnam draft dodgers. One of them, Muhammad Ali, beat the fearsome George Foreman in a huge Africa prizefight. *Happy Days* debuted on TV, and *Blazing Saddles* was a hit at the movies.

But on the ground in Boston, it was all about race and busing. Embracing the liberal social policies of the day, a federal judge named Arthur Garrity had ordered South Boston High School to be integrated. To achieve that end, it was decided that scores of black students were to be forcibly bused into the all-white school from distant neighborhoods. South Boston was (and is to this day) one tough neighborhood, dominated by working-class Irish and Italians who are generally suspicious of outsiders and of authority in general. Back in '74, Southie, as it is called, was entirely inhabited by white people, and most who lived there wanted it to stay that way.

So, after the judge proclaimed his busing order, blatant hatred took to the streets. There were threats and protests and major fear and loathing (Hunter S. Thompson's signature phrase). Everybody knew that when the first buses rolled into Southie, anything could happen, and all of it would be bad.

Through sheer persistence and hard work, I had become a columnist for the *Daily Free Press,* BU's student newspaper. That position gave me latitude to cover whatever I wanted. So early in the morning on integration day, I rode the T (Boston's tramway system) down to South Boston. It didn't take long for a major story to unfold. Here's how I described it in print:

> By 7:50 a.m. they were all assembled. Names like Conroy, O'Brien, Leary, LaRosa, and Mosso. Plenty of red-haired people with light skin and blue eyes. Young women with acne-infested complexions and thick thighs. Tough-looking boys wearing beach hats and patches of thin facial hair that might one day be beards. Toothless old women were there too, their sunken faces reflecting a life that refused to allow them the luxury of growing old gracefully. And, of course, the priests were there, trying futilely to calm their flawed flock. . . .
>
> At 8:05, the first bus arrived. Small black faces peered dumbfounded from behind bus windows. "F—— you, n——," someone yelled. The obscene chorus swelled. A rock hit the bus. The children were led safely off the vehicle by police, their eyes showing bewilderment and fear. But their confusion had not yet turned to hatred. . . .
>
> Out in the street, mothers wheeling babies yelled the vilest obscenities. Six-year-old children stood next to them echoing the filthy idioms. One kid was especially agitated.
>
> "How old are you?" I asked.
>
> "Thirteen."
>
> "You go to school?"
>
> "Yeah, but I ain't goin' 'til the n——s clear out."
>
> At that point, the kid's mother turned around.
>
> "Don't talk to him, Brian," she said. "Don't talk to anyone you don't know. If they're not from around here, don't have anything to do with them."

There was much more to my article, but you get the idea. The fact that I was witnessing history made a deep impression on me, and so did the unfairness of the situation. No American child should have been put in the position of the kids on those buses; both sides were desperately wrong. I was saddened that my people, the Irish, acted so hatefully toward innocent children. I was also furious that the federal system could not have found a better way to integrate schools. No sane government uses young kids as cannon fodder in an ideological war.

From that day on, I knew for certain that journalism would be my profession.

Thank God—and I mean that literally—I was given some writing and speaking ability. I was born with it. I have never taken a writing class or a public-speaking seminar. It was just there.

Now, I'm not a writer on the level of Norman Mailer or a speaker like Barack Obama, who is an amazing orator. But I can wield the pen and speak my mind without fear. These gifts were given to me, I believe, by a higher power. I respect my talent and try to use it for positive change, something I believe I have accomplished over my career.

Again, had I been sidetracked by trivial pursuits, had my brain been shrouded in a chemical fog, I would not have seen my vocation so clearly. I would not have been standing there on that warm September morning in South Boston. But I was there, and I will never forget it.

Sensing I might have nailed the busing story, I sent my article to journalist Pete Hamill, the legendary New York City–based newspaper columnist. I admired Hamill's work, and my father loved him. Like many students, I was looking for feedback. Unfortunately, Pete Hamill didn't know me at all, and I didn't expect a reply. But, a few weeks later, he sent me a very kind letter full of praise and advice.

That push from Pete gave me confidence and courage. Years later,

I ran into Hamill and told him that. We became friends. He's the man I most admire in print journalism.

Throughout that fall at BU, covering stories became a passion for me. I loved going places and seeing new things. I ran around Boston annoying the hell out of everyone, but bringing back good, crisp copy. In addition to the *Free Press,* I got stuff published in the *Boston Phoenix* and the *Real Paper.* Then, I recycled the articles into class assignments. Somehow, this worked out great. How could I get a bad grade if somebody had paid me for a piece and it ran on page two?

Full Exposure

Without a doubt, my most enjoyable story that semester was a meeting with the infamous stripper Fanne Foxe, aka "the Argentine Firecracker." This was huge because Ms. Fanne had become an international news sensation. At two in the morning on October 7, 1974, Democratic congressman Wilbur Mills, the powerful Ways and Means Committee leader from Ohio, was stopped by U.S. Park Police officers in Washington, D.C., because his chauffeur was driving with the headlights off. Later, authorities determined that Mills was drunk as the proverbial skunk.

As cops approached Mills's car that evening, a young woman leaped from the vehicle and ran into the nearby Tidal Basin, a swampy pool of water. Police chased her down and sent her to St. Elizabeths Hospital for observation.

The woman's name was Annabella Battistella, a thirty-eight-year-old striptease dancer from Argentina who performed under the name of Fanne Foxe, "the Argentine Firecracker." This entire incident, of course, did not look good for the married Mills, and naturally, the press went wild, labeling Ms. Battistella the "Tidal Basin Bombshell."

Fanne Foxe in a relatively demure moment.

While Mills went into damage-control mode, saying that he and the bombshell were just "friends," drinking buddies if you will, the resourceful Fanne went to work. Her agent immediately booked her on a cross-country strip tour, and one of the first stops was Boston.

Thank you, God.

On a cool November night, I ventured into Boston's notorious Combat Zone, a vice-ridden area just north of Boston Common. There, I met Ms. Bombshell backstage at the Pilgrim Theatre, where she was preparing to take off her clothes for three thousand dollars, a hefty one-night sum in 1974.

The woman was very nice to me and my photographer, Conn

O'Neill, two young Irish guys just trying to get through school. In fact, the Foxette actually changed into her costume right before our eyes, displaying an admirable female form. *Am I getting paid for this?* I thought. The answer was no. But it was okay.

Under my byline, the following words appeared the next day in the *Free Press*:

Ms. Foxe spoke with a soft Ricky Ricardo accent while talking about the infamous Mills incident. She put it this way: "Meester Mills took four of us out for dinner, dancing, and champagne at a nightclub in Washington. His wife had a hurt foot so she didn't come. I was sick with the flu and had been taking antibiotics, so after my *fifth* glass of champagne, I felt sick and dizzy.

"Normally, I don't drink hard liquor, maybe a leetle brandy once in a while, but five glasses of champagne would never get me drunk. It was the combination of the champagne and the antibiotics that made me dizzy.

"I don't remember much else. I panicked when the police stopped us and ran out. I didn't want to see the police. Meester Mills tried to stop me but my elbow hit his glasses and they broke, cutting his face. I got out of the car and, being dizzy, fell into the basin. That's all that happened."

Made sense to me. Like the Ghostbusters, I was ready to believe her.

So Fanne had her story and she was sticking to it. Who was I to argue? I wasn't there with her and the chairman of the House Ways and Means Committee. Had I been there, perhaps things would have turned out differently, as I would not have been drinking and always drive with the lights on. But, again, I was not there.

After about twenty minutes, I told Ms. Foxe I was grateful for her time and turned to leave. She smiled and hit me with this:

"I don't like to show 'everything,' but I think I'll keep on dancing for two years and then go to medical school."

Okay.

Out in the audience, I grabbed a seat as far away from the clientele as possible. My assignment was to cover Fanne Foxe, not get knifed. Here's how I summed up her performance:

Fanne whirls out onstage and in no time is down to her underwear. Like a jerk, I am wondering if she's going to show everything. Not only does she show everything, but also—the way she moves it around—the everything seems to walk off the stage and come over to sit on your lap. The crowd loves it.

After the everything has been shown . . . Fanne saunters around the stage bantering with the audience and throwing candy to the patrons. She asks one guy what kind of candy he wants.

"Whatever Wilbur Mills didn't eat," he screams.

Fanne laughs along with the rest of the politically aware audience, finishes her act, and bounces off the stage, everything still intact.

I guess you gotta make a living.

When my story appeared the next day, I thought it was a home run. But some of the feminists at the *Free Press* thought otherwise. The women's movement was just getting started and, truthfully, I was not engaged. Nor did I pretend to be. My first priority was finding out if I had talent, if I could cut it in the media world, not trying to figure out Betty Friedan.

So, seeking clarity on that front, I sent the Fanne piece to the feared movie reviewer Rex Reed, a guy who loathed many things and was not shy about saying so. Think Simon Cowell. I figured if Reed thought the piece was good, I knew I had something going in journalism.

A few days later, Rex Reed's letter arrived on *Chicago Tribune–New York News* stationery:

Dear Bill:

I think there's a solid future for you in journalism . . . that interview with Fanne Foxtail is simply great . . . better than anything that ran in the NY papers.

You really do have talent. I hope something good happens for you.

Years later, I told Rex Reed that he was directly responsible for my entering the field of mass communications and asked him if I should make that public.

He laughed and said he'd pay me not to.

What I learned at Boston University firmly set me on the course I continue to this day. Amidst the chaos of Commonwealth Avenue, I found an occupation that I enjoyed, that was noble (at least back then), and that I was certain was my vocational destiny.

To this day, I keep these lessons close:

- Work hard.
- Keep a clear head.
- Don't compromise when you know you're right.
- Give most people the benefit of the doubt.
- Don't fear authority.
- And definitely have a good time.

Destiny, I believe, played a role in my BU experience too. Here's my backup for that statement: in February 2008, a Harris Poll stated that I, the bold, fresh guy, had been selected the most-liked newsperson in the United States of America. Of course, back in the day, I never dreamed that would ever happen. But it has, and there are many people to blame. You know who you are.

8

STANDING FOR SOMETHING

He is happiest of whom the world says least, good or bad.

—THOMAS JEFFERSON (AUGUST 27, 1786)

My friend John Kasich, the former congressman from Ohio, wrote a book about standing for sincere principles that benefit society, and that work is far better than anything I could produce. But, in my life, being a "stand-up" person has, obviously, become paramount.

Thomas Jefferson, of course, did not take his own advice. He tried to do monumental things, and when you make that attempt, people are going to talk, and you are going to get hammered to some degree.

Anticipating that kind of acrimony, many people choose to sit it out. Whatever they believe, they keep it mostly to themselves. Play it safe. My parents certainly did that. So if that's true, how did I turn out to be a prime-time bloviator? To understand, we have to once again return along with the Lone Ranger and Tonto "to those thrilling days of yesteryear": Levittown in the 1950s.

On the night before my seventh birthday, September 9, 1956, Elvis Presley changed American society. The vehicle was *The Ed Sullivan Show,* where an astounding eighty-three percent of Americans who owned TV sets (about 54 million people) tuned in to see the rock phenom.

Presley sang "Hound Dog" and "Love Me Tender." My parents watched. My sister and I were already in bed. We missed some girls in the audience shrieking and Elvis grinning. Sullivan was his usual taciturn self.

What Elvis and the other rock pioneers did was alter American culture forever. Rock 'n' roll was not just music, but also an attitude full of rebellion and subversion against conformity and the prevailing wisdom of the 1950s. As Frankie Valli sang in the song "Grease," "Conventionality belongs to yesterday."

Under the rock music avalanche, the vanilla entertainment of Perry Como, Patti Page, and other crooners vanished as a dominant force, buried under lyrics and physical gyrations that put the fear of Satan into traditional parents. As the rock money came rolling in, much more provocative entertainment evolved, not only in music but also in books and movies. Elvis started it all on the mass-market level, even though he could never have known that back in '56.

My mother said she liked "Love Me Tender." Both parents gave the thumbs-down to "Hound Dog." Even so, despite harsh criticism about Elvis from religious people and politicians, my parents did not find Presley disturbing or corruptive. In my house, Elvis was tolerated, although rarely mentioned. But Jerry Lee Lewis and "Great Balls of Fire" were out, though, even before "the Killer" ran off to marry his thirteen-year-old cousin.

The indifference to Elvis was typical of my parents' reaction to most controversial things. At home, I heard little about the McCarthy hearings, or the Cold War, or even the Cuban Missile Crisis. My folks knew what was happening in the world, but did not feel compelled to comment.

Much later, I figured it out. Both of my parents were Depression kids, meaning they were raised in terrible economic times. When Franklin Delano Roosevelt took office in 1933, twenty-five percent of working-age Americans were unemployed. My dad was nine years old. In his Brooklyn neighborhood, hungry people stood in line for hours to get free food. For a young boy, the fear and suffering he saw in the adult world made a lasting impression. My grandfather did have a job as a New York police officer, but fear was in the air. Children were reared to obey and keep quiet. There was little joy in Mudville.

As he grew older, my father's world continued to be one of conformity. His stint as a naval officer during World War II imposed a dramatic discipline on him. Orders were to be obeyed, authority not questioned.

My mother was also ultracautious and rather complacent. Her childhood circumstances in Teaneck, New Jersey, were better than my father's, as both her parents had decent jobs. But constant uncertainty, and the paranoia that causes, deeply affected both of my parents. They became accepting adults, rarely questioning authority, almost never going against the prevailing wisdom.

In middle age, my father realized the downside of buying into complete conformity, but in my house the code never changed: To get along, you go along. Don't bring attention to yourself, don't rock any boats, save your money, and watch out for bad stuff, because you know it's coming down the pike. And above all else: DO NOT CAUSE TROUBLE!

So why didn't I get it?

My sister certainly did. Rabble-rousing was nowhere on her résumé. But her bold, fresh brother had a decidedly different point of view.

When I was a little kid, my independent streak (a kind description) was largely kept under control by constant activity. I was a leisure-time demon. A typical summer day might go like this:

- Get up, put on clothes, eat a bowl of Sugar Frosted Flakes with milk and slices of banana cut on top of it. Stare at picture of Tony the Tiger on cereal box, wondering how tigers eat Frosted Flakes. Do they have milk, spoons, and bowls in the jungle? Do they have grocery stores there? Do tigers have money to buy cereal? The questions are endless.

- Grab Davy Crockett coonskin cap, Fanner 50 six-guns and holster, and bolt out the door. Forget on purpose to brush teeth.

- March down the street and pound on Jimmy's door. "Can Jimmy come out and play?" I ask his mother. Of course. What sane adult would want Jimmy in the house? The kid is a walking disaster and a big-time dirt magnet.

- Jimmy and I then recruit three other urchins for trip to the woods a couple of blocks away. There, major shoot-outs take place, and massive amounts of dirt and debris relocate onto my clothing.

- Home for lunch, with Mom making me change clothes and "wash up." Bologna sandwich and Fritos appear. Food, such as it is, bolted down. Baseball hat and glove are procured.

- Stickball game ensues, with generally three fights over foul balls, high tags, and general disenchantment. Game usually dissolves when spaldeen (small, pink rubber ball) is hit into someone's bushes and the guy yells at us to stay off his lawn.

- Mom takes me and a couple of my thug friends to the Carmen Avenue swimming pool, a Levittown perk. Each housing development got a public pool so buyers could think they were living large.

• At least one fight breaks out in pool, usually over somebody doing a "cannonball" off the side and landing on another kid's head.

• Home to dry off and prepare for supper. TV goes on. *The Mickey Mouse Club* dominates, because my sister likes it and I am beginning to realize that Annette has a lot more going on besides fake ears.

• Supper. Often fish sticks, which are breaded and drowned with ketchup. Sometimes mashed potatoes accompany the delicious fish. Usually the potatoes come out of a box. When I ask my father about that, he says they taste better that way. Even I know that's stretching it.

• After dinner, play outside for an hour. The parental order is "be home when the streetlights come on." Early-evening activity often is ringolevio, where two teams of frenzied children try to maim one another for little apparent reason. Much clothing destroyed after supper.

• Bath time before bedtime. Hate this. Lava brand soap constantly in eyes, and what exactly is the point of cleanliness? Yes, it's next to godliness, but what the heck is that? No one in my circle knows.

• Lights-out at about nine, but sometimes, moments before, a late snack appears courtesy of my nice mother. These include Mallomars or Twinkies with milk. Sugar rush before bedtime leads to much tossing and turning before my father bellows, "Settle down before I come in there."

In short, the frenetic pace of my childhood prevented me from doing any real damage to others or myself. Those were the days when American kids pretty much did what they wanted in the play area until exhaustion set in. There were plenty of bikes, but no helmets. Lots of inventive games, but no "playdates." Ball games daily, usually without adult supervision except for the short Little League season.

So, for the entire first part of my life, I had largely unsupervised fun, and so did most of the other kids in my neighborhood. That environment will never be seen again in America, thanks to child predators and the Internet that has emboldened them.

The Class Factor

Alas, at age thirteen, I began to change. The year was 1962, and for the first time, I was associating with people who were far different than I was. Up until that first year of high school, every kid I knew was a working-class white person with two parents who lived in a small house that looked just like mine.

As I mentioned, I encountered blatant snobbery for the first time at Chaminade High. Some of my classmates looked down upon me, actually mocked me for my dress and mannerisms. And I wasn't alone; this kind of class-based hazing was rampant at the school.

At the same time, I was becoming somewhat aware of the outside world. In August 1962, Marilyn Monroe died, and that was a big deal, although I did not understand exactly why. Also, there was the ongoing tension between the USA and the Soviet Union. That I understood. The Russians were the bad guys. We Americans were the good guys. Kind of like the Green Bay Packers running over my New York Giants in the championship game that year. I understood bad guys.

Some of the ordinary guys at Chaminade tried to blend in with the cool segment, but I never did. I paraded my working-class pedigree around, and tough if you didn't like it. That was an important decision. To this day, I feel much more comfortable among the "folks." The "swells" hold little appeal for me.

But bucking the cool guys at Chaminade was no easy road. They came at me; I went right back at them. I saw other guys brutalized (mostly verbally) by these villains and not fighting back. But I did.

One quick story on this theme. The Chaminade football team was a perennial powerhouse on Long Island, and I thought I was good enough to make the squad. However, it was essentially a blue-blooded outfit, and the coach, a guy named Joe Thomas, had no room for me, even though I could punt, placekick, and throw the ball as well as anybody he had.

After Thomas told me to take a hike, I was teed off but not defeated. So I tried out for the ice hockey team. I wasn't as good at hockey as I was at football, but the team needed a goalie, and I would throw myself in front of speeding pucks all day long. I mean, why not?

One problem: goalie stuff. An ice hockey goaltender needs an enormous amount of expensive equipment, from leg pads to special gloves to the all-important protective mask. That cost money, which I didn't have. So I improvised. A friend of mine gave me a lacrosse mask. I "liberated" (Leninist term meaning "stole") a baseball chest protector from my summer team, and my mother sewed a knee-pad onto the bottom of my first-baseman's mitt to create a goalie's catching glove. Perhaps feeling a bit guilty watching the bizarre assemblage, my father then ponied up twenty-five bucks for some fourth-hand leg pads.

To say I looked a bit unusual is to say Boy George is a strange

A rare appearance outside the goal!

guy. You think? I was Herman Munster on skates. But *I did not care.*
I started in goal, and the Chaminade ice hockey team made the play-
offs. It's not how you look; it's how you play, baby.

By my senior year, I had made relative peace with the school,
even though I had developed the edge in my personality that I have
to this day. Simply put, no one was going to push me around, and
I would challenge authority if I felt it was oppressive. That was my
game plan.

Even though I found success in hockey, the football thing still
nagged at me. One day after the football season ended, some of
the players were bragging about their athletic prowess. After about
thirty seconds, I got fed up with hearing it and issued a clear chal-

lenge: my neighborhood guys can kick your butts on the football field!

Okay. Game on.

It was a cold December Saturday in 1966 when members of the Chaminade High School football team showed up in Levittown to play my sandlot team. But, like a smart college coach, I had been recruiting. My fullback, Gary Kliss, had a cousin in Virginia who was six-foot-six. Presto, he became a Levittown guy, y'all. Also, I brought in a couple of ringers from the local public school team. We were ready.

The Chaminade guys wore their nifty red-and-yellow jerseys. We wore gray sweatshirts and jeans. They had cleats. We had sneakers. They were overconfident; we had attitude.

Stunningly, my father had volunteered to ref the game, because I think he feared a major brawl was going to break out. There was certainly that feeling in the air. He and another Chaminade father stood on the field and kept relative order.

Back then, we played tackle football without equipment. Not even a cup. It was really rugby, and it was brutal.

Of course, I was the quarterback. Early on, I pitched out to Joey Dalton, who promptly fumbled. My father sauntered over and quietly said, "Joey's scared; get him out of there."

Done. By the way, Joey was smart to be petrified. The game was a slaughterhouse. Kind of like the movie *The Longest Yard*. Guys limped off the field or were dragged off after almost every play. By halftime, I saw some Chaminade guys looking over to our sideline and staring. There was blood in the dirt. This was genuine class warfare, no question.

My guys knew it. They badly wanted to win this game, and we did. The final score was 24–14. After my father blew the final whistle, one Chaminade guy said, "Let's keep playing." I thought both teams would beat him to a pulp.

The game is still talked about back in Levittown, more than forty years after the fact.

From that time on, I've always been on the side of the underdog. Anyone watching me on television knows that. I want everyday folks to get a fair shot and the powerful to be held accountable. I believe cops, firefighters, teachers, and the military are practicing noble professions and are the backbone of the nation.

It's not that I dislike the white-wine crew; I don't. But I'm uncomfortable hanging with them. I don't want to explain the songs of Herman's Hermits or the appeal of Charles Bronson. No, I'm happy using my skills and power to stand up for the folks, people with whom I have much in common. At my age, I don't want to learn a new skill set. If I see four forks at the dinner table, I know I'm in the wrong place.

Summing up this chapter, I stand solidly for self-reliance but realize that a fair social and economic system is necessary to complement that. If somebody is getting special privileges, I want to know why. Because of my philosophy, I have taken on some powerful entities in America and have won most of my battles. But like that Saturday football game, it's been a rough fight; there has been blood, as Daniel Day-Lewis well knows.

This is not a self-congratulatory analysis. I could have gone another way and there wouldn't have been anything wrong with that. After getting a master's degree from Harvard, I had more than a few opportunities to earn money representing "polite society." I turned them down. My mission lay elsewhere. My upbringing demanded it.

While I was working as a correspondent for ABC News (a definite blue-blood outfit), my friend, the late Peter Jennings, wanted to send me to work in the London bureau to "round out the rough edges." I told him no thanks, that I wanted to keep the edges. He politely told me I was nuts, because London, back then, was a fast-track bureau in the world of network news. Peter Jennings himself had achieved stardom while working out of the London bureau. But it was not right for me, and I knew it.

By the way, without his ever stating it, I believe Peter respected the fact that I was loyal to my roots. When I wrote a piece in *Newsweek* magazine about working-class Americans who had become wealthy, Jennings asked me to do a report on the article for *World News Tonight.* That stunned some of the snobby Ivy Leaguers who worked for him.

Years later, when Peter saw what I was doing with *The O'Reilly Factor,* he called me, saying the "edges" had indeed paid off. "But I could never do what you do," Jennings said.

I told him I understood that. Peter was a good guy at heart, but he was a patrician. I really respected him, but I didn't want to be like him. I couldn't say the word *shan't* no matter how hard I tried.

Hey, I'm a Levittown guy, and that's what I stand for.

Okay?

CHAPTER 9

CONSERVATIVES VERSUS LIBERALS

One nation under God, indivisible.
—THE PLEDGE OF ALLEGIANCE

N ot too many liberals lived in my Levittown neighborhood; this was not a place for progressives. Many of the denizens were former military, and almost all had attended the school of hard knocks. That meant money was usually tight and the work hours long. Under that atmosphere, liberal programs like tax-funded entitlements for the unemployed and sympathy for permissive behavior were not eagerly embraced. In fact, in the seventeen years I lived there, I knew only two people who actually leaned left.

Both were mothers of my friends.

Sheila M. was a *New York Times*–reading, Adlai Stevenson–loving leftie. She was also one of the nicest moms in town. A brunette with a perpetual smile, Sheila was loved by us kids because she let us run wild on her property. While most parents shrieked loudly when children roughed up their beloved bushes or shrubs, Sheila could not have cared less. Thus, her lawn became ground zero for violent, mindless games like "keep-away."

I pledge Allegiance to the Flag of the United States of America and to the Republic for which it Stands: One Nation under God, Indivisible, with Liberty and Justice for All.

My St. Brigid's autograph book opens with this page.

Picture two teams of crazed ten-year-old boys—five on each side. A football is thrown into the air and, as it falls, one team tries to grab it and keep possession, while the other team tries to take the ball away. There are no rules; anything goes. There is no scoring, no winners or losers. There is only mayhem as we ruffians knock one another stupid trying to either get the ball or keep the ball.

In winter, we played this dumb game nearly every day.

Of course, Sheila's lawn and surrounding shrubbery were quickly destroyed. I'm talking total annihilation, nuclear-winter stuff. No way my father would have allowed that on our tiny property. In fact, nobody's parents would have it. Only Sheila M. gave us free rein.

Much later, when we were talking about the old days, one of Sheila's sons told me she simply believed that kids having fun trumped any sod considerations. Sheila was from the "Summerhill" school of child rearing, whereby the youngster's "creative" aspirations are all-important. Developed by a man named A. S. Neill, Summerhill is an actual school in England where the kids pretty much do whatever they want short of witch burning. In that permis-

sive atmosphere, the controversial theory goes, children will grow
into loving and responsible adults because they have not been traumatized by "restrictions." I do not believe there have ever been any
nuns at Summerhill.

However, there was a downside to Sheila's liberal child-raising
point of view: cursing. She didn't do it, but her eldest son, Robert,
did it with gusto. While most of us were commanded under threat
of punishment not to take the Lord's name in vain or use the F-word,
Robert would let profanity fly pretty much anytime he felt like it.
My mother was appalled.

But, according to sworn testimony from her three kids, Sheila felt
that cursing was just a stage that some children went through. Fine
with me. Not fine with most of the other parents. There was some
tension over this.

The other liberal mom in the neighborhood was Kay, also a very
nice woman. Short and thin with light-colored hair, Kay was the
mother of Genie and Stu, two kids I met at age three. Unfortunately,
Kay was a "lapsed Catholic," which meant she did not practice the
faith. You'll not be surprised to hear that this was not good in Levittown, as most Catholics did not approve of any lapsing. Both St.
Brigid's and St. Bernard's churches were packed every Sunday, but
Kay, her husband, Genie, and Stu were never sighted. One time I
asked Stu where his family went to church, and he told me they
didn't have to go because they were "Unitarian." This sounded good
to me, but when I broached the subject with my parents at dinner,
the conversation did not go far.

Even so, my mother and father were remarkably kind whenever
they discussed Kay. My parents were not big on passing judgment
unless it involved me. Then judgment was passed with stunning
speed.

Anyway, like Sheila, Kay was okay with kid conduct that other
parents would never have permitted. One day, armed with water
pistols, a few of us showed up at Kay's house and proceeded to

douse Genie in a major way. In response, he got buckets of water and drenched us. We then chased young Gene *into his own home,* and a massive water fight erupted, causing some visible damage. During this conflict, Kay was across the street at neighbor Betty's house and, upon returning home, found sodden furniture and actual puddles on the floor.

Kay just stared. Guilty as sin, we thought all hell would break loose. But no, she calmly ordered us out of the house and closed the front door. The next day I asked Genie exactly what his mother did to him.

"Not much," the kid replied. "She just said our conduct was inappropriate."

Wow. What a mom!

Both Sides Now

Singer Judy Collins had a big hit with a Joni Mitchell song that said she looked at life from both sides. Well, I never got that chance in my childhood. There was only one side: conservative. It was dominant.

So, the Russians were bad, as were Castro and all communist "agitators." Truth be told, my gang agitated far more than any communist could have, but we did it while loving America. On the Fourth of July, everybody flew the flag and went to a picnic. John Wayne and Audie Murphy were huge in the movies, and the blond, wholesome Doris Day was prettier than any woman on earth. Are we clear about this?

That was why the late 1960s were so shocking for many of us in the neighborhood. For the first time in my life, America was being portrayed as bad. That was unheard-of in Levittown. But the Vietnam War battered conventional thinking, and within a very short period of time, some kids who were once vocal right-wingers grew their hair long and started thinking Abbie Hoffman, cofounder of the Youth International Party (the yippies), was a cool guy.

I, the bold, fresh guy, did not fall into that trap.

Perhaps because politics basically bored me, I did not get emotionally involved with the "Chicago Seven," Jane Fonda's crew, or any other hysteria. In 1967, I did begin following the Vietnam controversy, but only from a distance. I kept my emotions out of it. That summer, I was still in an all-American, 1950s state of mind, lifeguarding for spending money and training hard for the upcoming football season. But even in the barbecue haze of the suburbs, it was hard not to notice the Beatles morphing from clean-cut guys to wild-eyed "All You Need Is Love" gurus. Thank God Elvis didn't crack.

Unfortunately, as many kids changed their look and style, some adults began badly misbehaving, overreacting to antiwar protests and the rapidly changing culture. I heard a lot of hateful stuff that summer from middle-aged adults who condemned good men like Dr. Martin Luther King Jr. and others who were considered rabble-rousers.

That behavior disturbed me as much as seeing some of my friends stoned on whatever they could get. I never got the antiblack thing. New York Giants center fielder Willie Mays was my guy even after the team moved to San Francisco. Cleveland Browns running back Jim Brown was actually from Long Island. I idolized these men. So when some adults threw the N-word around and mocked blacks, I had a hard time processing it. If all races were cheering blacks on the field—and they were—why would anyone deride that race after the game? The antiblack crew in the neighborhood could never answer that simple question.

Levittown, by design, was all white. The real estate agents simply would not sell to blacks. There was no religious restriction, as Jews and Christians lived side by side, but the blacks in the area lived in a neighborhood called New Cassell, a few miles away. We never went there.

As racial tensions rose along with the Vietnam chaos, I finally asked my father about it. Both he and my grandfather, a New York City police officer, never bashed blacks in front of me. I never heard that. Once in a while, another group might get slighted, but not black people.

I mentioned the following story briefly in *Culture Warrior,* but I think it's worth repeating in this context. As we sat on the small back patio of our house on a humid evening, my father told me that some folks in our neighborhood had experienced difficulties with blacks in Brooklyn or the Bronx. Many Levittown people were raised in those New York City boroughs and had moved out when the minorities moved in.

My father told me that real estate predators, exploiting fear and racism, would buy single-family homes and then illegally rent them to multiple families of minorities, mostly blacks and Puerto Ricans. Almost immediately, entire blocks in New York City were impacted. Once new minority faces appeared, some white families panicked (which was the strategy) and sold their homes to these "blockbuster" real estate guys at very low prices. Whereupon the cycle would continue: minorities in, whites out. Thus, in a relatively short period of time, whole neighborhoods changed from ethnic white to "colored," as they said back then. My father thought the "blockbusters" were despicable, but some of my Levittown neighbors blamed the minorities themselves for the "white flight" epidemic.

So, as the late sixties roared on, both sides held little attraction for me. The conservative side was angry and sometimes bigoted, and the liberal side was equally angry and often hateful toward their own country. With neither choice appealing, I remained on the sidelines, swimming and running, huffing and puffing.

Looking back, I'm glad I stayed unaligned. I have never been a follower; I've always thought for myself. Lots of folks across the country lost their minds, and some their lives, back in those turbulent Vietnam War years, but I actually kept some perspective. Chalk one up for me.

As for the liberal-versus-conservative deal, the culture war never really erupted in Levittown. Sheila and Kay were the exceptions, as most everybody in the area remained conservative Republican. In fact, the GOP dominated Nassau County right up to the turn of the twenty-first century. Then the entrenched, arrogant Republican machine blew up. Not because of ideology, but because massive corruption was exposed. But to this day, Levittown is working-class-hero territory. Few there are exploring a move to San Francisco.

As for me, the bold, fresh guy, I am now branded a conservative by some in the crazed, dishonest, ultraliberal media, and do you know what? That's fine with me. As stated, I hold many traditional, conservative views and am proud of them. My problem-solving abilities are based on fairness, hard work, and honesty, and are not located in some theoretical comfort zone. That's why I win most of my debates on TV and radio. I deal in tough reality, not wishful thinking.

Let me expand on that with a simple example that even the dreamer Jimmy Carter might understand. The solution to poverty is not sympathy. That makes the sympathizer feel good but does little to help the guy who needs money. No, the solution to poverty in America is to say, "Hey, go back to school, learn a skill, and work hard when somebody hires you."

And, in our society, just about every American has the opportunity to do that. Excuses walk.

But noooooo (sorry, Belushi). Pinheads keep saying that I'm wrong. Poverty is society's fault . . . right, John Edwards? He claims there are two Americas, one for rich guys like him and me (who somehow magically acquired money) and one for the poor people whom the evil government has singled out to be hosed. That line of thinking is pure quackery—a false premise from the jump, no hard evidence to back it up.

As we discussed in the Katrina chapter, individual responsibility is the key to success in life. But, as teaching at Pace High School taught me, some individuals will avoid taking that responsibility;

for whatever reason they will hurt themselves and others. Most of the time, I blame them, not America. That, of course, separates me from the left and makes me a mean guy in their eyes.

Not that I care; I don't. My vast experience in life makes the following analysis easy, so listen up. Many liberals simply want to feel good about *themselves.* Showing compassion to the downtrodden accomplishes that. So it's not about the poor; it's about the liberal thinker. He or she wants to feel noble. The math here is pretty clear. If you blame someone for his or her own difficult circumstances, that's a harsh assessment, not a feel-good proposition. But if you blame a country or a system, and give the individual a free pass, then you are understanding and kind.

But think about it: what good does that really do? Of course, some poor people deserve pity, but far more would benefit from instruction and discipline. Look at the 1996 Welfare Reform Act signed by Bill Clinton. (By the way, the official title of the law is "The Personal Responsibility and Work Opportunity Reconciliation Act." Get it?) Many liberals screamed about its supposed unfairness. But studies show it helped far more Americans than it hurt. Forcing people to work led to millions of Americans entering the capitalist system, where they could actually accomplish something. Of course, that benefited both the individual and society. Did John Edwards miss that?

No, Edwards didn't miss it. He just wanted to play to the far-left crowd in his dismal run for the presidency. What a charlatan. And one more thing. If you see Edwards or any of his ideological soul mates, tell them this: In 1960, just five percent of American babies were born out of wedlock. Now, thirty-five percent are. And for African Americans, the number is an astounding seventy percent. That's what drives poverty, single-mother homes. Individual Americans having children they cannot afford to raise is the primary cause of poverty in the United States. That's a fact. And here's another fact: John Edwards and his ilk are pinheads. No doubt.

A Maalox Moment

Because I choose my friends based upon their characters and not ideology, I have a number of liberal pals with whom I can honestly discuss issues like what drives poverty. Recently, I was in Los Angeles having dinner with a friend of mine who is big on universal health care. She is really jazzed about the government providing medical care to "all who need it."

So the bold, fresh guy, in between bites of calamari, surgically took her opinion apart. Great friend, right? First, I asked her if Americans had a constitutional right to health care. Being of the liberal persuasion, of course she said yes. Okay.

Then I asked, if good health is indeed a protected right, shouldn't nutritious food be provided as well? After all, one cannot have good health without good food.

Being a smart lady, she saw the chess move and said she'd have to think about that. But the bold, fresh guy was moving in; nothing could stop me, not even the Dover sole that the waiter placed in front of me.

"Why do you have to think about it?" I asked. "You can't separate nutrition from health. Can't be done. So, by your way of thinking, the government has an obligation to provide good food to ensure good health for those who need it, right?"

"Maybe," she answered, chewing her sushi a bit more aggressively.

"Okay," I said. "And how about decent housing? If you live in substandard housing, it will definitely affect your health, no question. Right?"

At this point, my friend smiled, because she is a great person with no rancor and freely chooses to undergo grillings like this from her misguided friend (me).

"Sure, good food, good housing, it's all tied in," she said.

"And the government should provide those things to the poor?"

"Yes."

"Well, you're a socialist."

She smiled wider. "I guess I am," she said.

"That means I'll have to pick up the check," I replied. "Want dessert?"

You can see why dinner with me is not exactly on the menu for many people. But I'm right when I say that the left wants a big-daddy government to "provide." The problem is, that's impossible in America. If you don't believe me, recall your personal bureaucratic nightmare when trying to get a passport or a driver's license. And you want the government telling you which doctor to go to? Come on.

Independent thinkers like me realize that government safety nets must be provided for folks who cannot, for whatever reason, negotiate life on their own. That is realistic compassion. But in a nation of 300 million people, the government simply cannot "provide" for your needs. It is truly impossible.

Instead, creative programs like tax-free medical savings accounts and deregulation of the health insurance industry (with strict rules and oversight by the authorities) are the best solutions to the chaotic health care problem. But the left is generally not onboard with that.

Not to belabor left-wing blind spots, but I have to return to my pal John Edwards one last time before I move on to some conservative failings. On January 3, 2008, Edwards first claimed that two hundred thousand U.S. veterans were homeless and abandoned, sleeping under bridges because the economy was stacked against them. How could the USA allow that to happen? Edwards wailed. What is wrong with our country?

Now, this sounded a bit fishy to me, so I asked the Fox News "brain room" to check it out. That's the research arm of Fox Newschannel, and those guys are good. Quickly, the information came back: there were no accurate counts of homeless vets, just estimates by some veterans organizations that are dependent on donations to exist. Thus, they had a vested interest in putting out high homeless vet numbers. There was also no reliable economic data on homeless vets, but Joseph Califano, who heads a substance-abuse think tank at Columbia University, estimated that ninety percent of homeless vets are either addicted or mentally ill.

And the stats just kept on coming. The "brain room" found out that the Department of Veterans Affairs provides 150,000 beds each evening of the year for vets who need shelter. Agency workers will even pick up the vets and take them to facilities. Finally, the U.S. government is now spending a record amount of money on health programs for vets in all areas.

After I made all of those facts known, Edwards went on David Letterman's program and, in the ensuing discussion, agreed with Dave that I was lying about the vets. The candidate insisted yet again that the economy was forcing vets to live on the streets, and Dave, being the committed liberal that he is, enthusiastically agreed. Well, the whole controversy soon became moot for Edwards. A few days after his Letterman appearance, he dropped out of the presidential sweepstakes and returned to his $6-million, approximately thirty-thousand-square-foot home on a hundred and two North Carolina acres.

"Two Americas," indeed.

So you tell me, is it not difficult to respect the false premises that left-wing loons like Edwards put out there? Or am I wrong? By the way, for all the yammering on the left about increased government spending on social programs for the poor, studies show that conservative religious people give far more to charity per capita than secular-progressives.

The truth hurts, right, progressive people?

Might Makes Right

Staunch conservatives often are resistant to change, by definition. In 1960s Levittown, skepticism greeted most new trends, until, of course, they reached critical mass. I'd say we were generally at least a year behind what was happening socially in California, and some things have never caught on. Like gelato.

Now, sometimes failing to change for the sake of change is good. Caution is not a bad thing. But sometimes conservatives, like their left-wing counterparts, can be terribly wrong.

Here's a good example. In 1986, President Ronald Reagan, by far the most admired conservative in the country right now, allowed about three million illegal aliens amnesty, and then did little to stop millions of other foreign nationals from entering the United States illegally in the wake of his beneficent citizenship action. Subsequently, Presidents Bush, Clinton, and Bush the younger all followed Reagan's lead and avoided confronting the illegal-alien issue. Of course, disaster ensued. Estimates are that there could be as many as 15 million people living in the United States illegally, causing financial and social chaos in many parts of the country.

In addition, five of the nineteen 9/11 killers were in this country illegally, and, despite that, it is still relatively easy to sneak into America for whatever purpose.

Now, you would think conservative leaders would have aggressively tried to control the illegal immigration situation, but they obviously did not. Big business wanted cheap labor, and so the right did the wrong thing: they acquiesced to business and failed to act.

Likewise on oil. My father worked for Chevron (the parent corp. of Caltex) and told me in the 1960s that the Arabs had the USA over a barrel (sorry). Anybody with a brain knew that cheap foreign oil was a powder keg. That's one of the reasons why Japan started World War II, to secure oil supplies in Southeast Asia. But conservative presidents from Eisenhower to Bush the younger did little to develop alternative fuel or encourage conservation and better fuel standards for American automobiles. Now all of us are paying big-time for that sellout.

And while we're on the subject, one of the reasons that Al Gore has never agreed to be interviewed by me is that he knows I would ask him why he didn't push alternative fuel and conservation in the eight years he was vice president. The record shows that the Clinton administration was abysmal in this area. What say you, Mr. Gore?

Maybe ol' Al had an epiphany after he left office; his global warming quest might have changed his perspective. Fine. But Clinton-Gore had plenty of time to pound the alternative fuel drum and did not.

And speaking of global warming, some conservatives are nitwits on this subject, are they not? My take again is simple: only the Deity knows if the current warming trend on earth is man-made or part of a long-term natural cycle. To debate the cause of global warming is a complete waste of time. Again, NO ONE KNOWS why; we just know the earth's temperature is up. Are you hearing me?

But what all sane people *should* know is that clean air and water are good things, right? Eating fish contaminated with mercury is not my idea of fine dining. So shouldn't we all be demanding that governments clean up their countries and stop the madness? Why is pollution control an ideological issue?

Okay, let's transition into more ideological idiocy. Crazed ideologues on the right who laugh off environmental concerns are just as stupid as crazed ideologues on the left who have somehow determined that human life in the womb is expendable.

Just as with global warming, no one knows exactly when life begins. Only the Deity knows. You can *believe* anything you want, but you DON'T KNOW. We do know one thing, however: scientists have proven that upon conception, human DNA is present. Get it? The fetus already has the codes in place from its biological mother and father. So the "mass of nonhuman cells" argument goes right out the window if you're an honest person.

In my opinion, the "compassionate" liberal cadre that supports abortion on demand—for any reason at any time—is guilty of gross human-rights violations. Worshiping at the altar of "reproductive rights" is wrong. Abortion should be rare, regulated, and discouraged. Human dignity demands it.

So you can see that the bold, fresh guy has some problems with both sides of the ideological spectrum. But unlike Judy Collins, who sang about not knowing life at all, I am more confident in my views. Independent thought based upon greater good, realism, and, yes, compassion drives my agenda and dictates my analysis.

Two more things. Some conservatives are moralists; that is, they frame their opinions within the concept of "sin." That's a loser all day long, despite the fact that Sister Lurana would have pummeled me for saying it.

Let's go back to the out-of-wedlock birth rate. I've heard right-wing commentators condemn this situation on moral grounds, saying the people in this situation are guilty of sinful behavior. But why bother with that line of thinking when secular-progressives, who are loath to make moral judgments, are not likely to listen?

Instead, why not continually point to poverty? Virtually every study ever done on the poor in America says that homes run by single mothers have a much higher chance of being destitute than homes with a mom and a dad. This is undeniable and crushes all liberal arguments against the traditional family unit.

When the living-together and babies-out-of-wedlock trend began to challenge traditional marriage in the late sixties, few liberals foresaw the decline of the family that subsequently has led to enormous social problems. And right there is the big problem with committed liberal thought: the quest for individual gratification, for self-expression above responsibility to others, often has huge unintended consequences.

"If it makes you feel good" sounded great coming from Janis Joplin, remember?

She died at age twenty-seven from a drug overdose. I bet it would feel a lot better to be alive today.

CHAPTER 10

HEROES AND ZEROS

No man is justified in doing evil on the ground of expediency.
—THEODORE ROOSEVELT

Closing in on age eleven in the summer of 1960, I became a more creative hell-raiser (Summerhill would be proud). Using my organizational skills, my gang gathered for nighttime raids that included kicking over full garbage cans and swimming in people's pools under the cover of darkness. We did it purely for fun and it was harmless. Annoying, but harmless.

The big pop hit that summer was Brian Hyland's "Itsy Bitsy Teenie Weenie Yellow Polka-Dot Bikini," which blared daily from the loudspeakers at the Carmen Avenue swimming pool. WABC radio, the big New York rock station, spun the bikini song every hour on the hour, driving more than a few parents underwater. But I liked the song very much, especially the finale:

From the locker to the blanket,
From the blanket to the shore,

From the shore to the water,
Guess there isn't any more.

Is that poetry or what?

In the cinema, there was an Alfred Hitchcock movie called *Psycho* that my parents would not let me see. This was disturbing. It couldn't be any worse than *Not of This Earth,* could it? Besides, the ads said that the theater had a nurse standing by in case anybody passed out from fright (I'm not making this up), but my folks would not give in. They might already have one junior psycho on their hands; they didn't need Hitchcock to further the situation.

Many days that summer, we played stickball on the hot pavement of Levittown's Patience Lane, because a ton of kids lived on the poorly named street. You see, some adults residing on Patience Lane had absolutely no patience whatsoever, and in early July, an interesting little skirmish broke out.

At issue was the little ball itself. Often, it was being hit onto lawns. That required fielders to leave the public street and chase the ball onto private property. Many adults on Patience Lane ignored the trespass, but some did not. The worst offender was Mr. D., a tall, balding guy with a dour disposition.

If you can believe it, that guy actually confiscated the ball when it rolled onto his lawn. Let me repeat that: *The guy took the ball!*

Of course, that could not stand.

As mentioned earlier, our balls, called spaldeens, were small and bouncy and cost about ten cents each. By taking the ball, Mr. D. was costing us money, but that wasn't the big issue. No, the major point of contention concerned a unilateral hostile action against us kids. It was the principle involved. Even though we were not quite clear why, my gang was big on principle.

So Mr. D. had to pay.

Now, you might be asking why we didn't go to our parents and have them negotiate with Mr. D. for the return of the ball. A perfectly logical, but naive question. Back then, parents stuck together. Rarely, if ever, would a parent side with a kid against an adult. It was some kind of demented antikid code. Plus, technically, Mr. D. was correct: my stickball teammates and I had no legal right to trample his lawn. So we deemed parental intervention to be a loser and never even considered it. Instead, vigilante justice, widely admired among my set, was put into motion. (Kids today, of course, could read my recent book about the rights of children, *Kids Are Americans Too,* and come up with a smarter approach. But that summer, we were on our own.)

Because the Mr. D. revenge operation was a nighttime play, let me set the tactical scene. My bedroom was the only one upstairs in the O'Reilly house. My sister and parents slept on the ground floor. Often in the summer, it was ungodly hot upstairs. Air-conditioning? Are you kidding me? Only rich people could afford that. To stop my whining, my father did eventually buy me a small fan, but when I pointed out that it simply blew the humid air into my face that much quicker, he replied in his usual pithy way, "So don't use it."

Okay.

Back then, most everybody in Levittown left all the doors and windows open in the summertime, hoping that an occasional breeze would waft in through the screens. That made it easy for me to silently walk down the stairs and exit undetected through the back door of my house at any time during the night. Piece of cake.

This tactical advantage was key to Operation Mr. D., and here's how it went down: I had an old alarm clock in my room that rang so loudly dogs would file charges. The hellish thing was so annoying, I never used it. Not only was it loud, but the ringing also went on forever. This was a perfect nocturnal weapon.

I believe it was a Thursday night, but I could be wrong about that. I also believe four of us met up at Sheila's house at around one in the morning, but that too might be a misty watercolored memory, as Barbra Streisand once sang. But no matter, it was late on a weeknight when little Dave, the most agile climber, scooted up the tree outside Mr. D.'s upstairs bedroom and taped the alarm clock to a branch just a few feet away from his open window.

The alarm was set to go off fifteen minutes after Dave began his climb.

Mission accomplished, Dave scampered down, and we all hid in the bushes outside of Sheila's house, which was almost directly across the street from Mr. D.'s place. We absolutely had to watch our plan play out. I remember those waiting moments were very, very long until, finally, the alarm rang . . . and rang . . . and RANG!

Lights snapped on not only in Mr. D.'s house, but also inside a number of other homes on the block. Suddenly, adults appeared outside. They looked annoyed. We were thrilled.

Because it was dark, no one could pinpoint the shrieking alarm that made the Energizer Bunny look comatose. As it continued ringing, we stifled laughter in our hideout. Then, suddenly, we heard increasingly loud voices.

"Someone call the police!"

Uh-oh.

That was our cue to slither out of the bushes and run quickly to our respective homes. I made it to mine in record time, a mass of perspiration covering my entire body. Ever so quietly, I ascended the stairs, pulled off my sweaty, dirty clothes, hid them in the crawl space in the attic abutting my room, and climbed into bed.

Just in time to hear sirens.

From what we heard the next day, the cops showed up shortly after the alarm clock died. Their powerful flashlights located it, prompting one simple question: who could have done this?

Hi.

But there was no proof; even better, there at least a dozen stickball-playing suspects. Bottom line: we were never apprehended.

Of course, Mr. D. suspected who the culprits were and took his case to our parents, but we vigorously denied any and all wrong-doing, thereby committing a series of sins that I confessed to Father Ellard a few days later. However, with evidence scarce, the caper soon died, even though my father thought the clock that Mr. D. showed him looked familiar.

I was thankful my dad didn't pursue the matter—mainly, I believe, because he thought Mr. D. was a doofus.

Now, I am telling you this story because it epitomizes my attitude about heroes and villains. I was always much more interested in bringing the villains down than in celebrating the heroes. To this day, that is my attitude.

It's not that I don't respect and admire heroes; I do. Abraham Lincoln, Franklin Roosevelt, Bobby Kennedy, Winston Churchill, George Washington, Mother Teresa, Bono, and hundreds of others are an important part of my personal history. I've taken the time to learn about them and, in various situations, I try to emulate their courage and foresight. But I am obsessed with hammering villains.

Maybe it's because of the excitement factor. I mean, Saint Francis of Assisi was a great guy with the animals, birds, and such. But Saint Michael the Archangel was *really* impressive, wielding that big sword to chase the demons back into hell, where they certainly belonged.

In fact, I took Michael as my confirmation name. (This is a Catholic ritual in which you choose an additional name for yourself that reconfirms your baptism into the faith as an infant. The theory is that babies can't choose to be Catholic, but twelve-year-olds can. Especially with a menacing nun in proximity.)

All my early heroes were villain bashers: Davy Crockett righting those wrongs on the frontier and at the Alamo. Wyatt Earp taking no garbage from those Tombstone bad guys. Eliot Ness chasing down Al Capone, a very mean guy whose nasty facial scar just reinforced the point. The list was very long. To this day, I identify with and support folks who fight against evildoers.

But there is one small problem with my attitude: You'd better be sure you know who really deserves a bit of retribution, because if you make a mistake major damage can result. This is real life, not a Charles Bronson *Death Wish* movie. I take the chasing villains deal very seriously, and always have.

Back in the day, Mr. D. certainly deserved the jazz we gave him. I have no problem with that caper. The man got what he deserved in a creative, relatively harmless manner. By the way, after we disturbed his slumber, Mr. D. kept a much lower profile in the neighborhood. He didn't interrupt any more stickball games.

If you watch the *Factor* these days, you know that we often "ambush" bad guys: that is, we arrive with cameras rolling and confront them with tough questions. Remember Michael Nifong, that irresponsible North Carolina prosecutor? We confronted him on the air months before he was convicted of railroading those Duke lacrosse players in a phony rape beef.

Also, we nailed Rosie O'Donnell on her nutty 9/11 conspiracy theory that bombs located inside the structure destroyed one of the World Trade Center buildings. A study by engineers at Purdue University blew O'Donnell out of the water, and I made sure everybody knew about it.

And, in a great piece of reporting, we hammered NBC News/*Washington Post* analyst William Arkin after this pinhead guy called American troops serving in Iraq "mercenaries." We confronted the guy in Massachusetts, and he ran like the coward he is.

To some, a TV ambush is a controversial technique, but I believe it is absolutely necessary. We live in a time when powerful people can hide behind hired spinners and concrete walls, evading scrutiny for evil deeds. Villains can easily say "no comment" and avoid explaining their destructive actions. This is not okay.

For example, let's take judges who sentence convicted child molesters to probation, no prison time. That was going on to a disturbing degree in Vermont, as I documented in *Culture Warrior*. Well, we confronted two of those judges, the most reprehensible of the lot, and the entire country saw them run away rather than explain their irresponsible sentences. Good.

But be assured: my staff vigilantly researched those men before we traveled to Vermont to confront them in person. We examined their sentencing histories; we gave them every chance to explain themselves. They passed, so we paid them a visit.

We have done that scores of times over the years, and guess what? Dozens of prosecutors have written to me saying that formerly lenient judges have changed their, well, points of view. In fact, after we exposed those Vermont judges, the lenient sentences for child abusers pretty much stopped in the Green Mountain State.

That's because most villains are cowards, they do their bad deeds feeling they are immune from retaliation. Nowhere is this more evident than in the corrupt American media.

We Bring Good Things to Light

Let me back up that statement with a vivid example of what I consider to be villainy in the media. I am doing this because I feel very strongly that some in the media are abusing their constitutionally guaranteed privileges. It is flat-out wrong to hide behind the First Amendment while doing dishonest, destructive things. That wasn't the intent of the Founding Fathers. I think most everyone would agree with that.

Thus, I feel that the powerful villains who allow media corruption should be exposed. By the way, I could harpoon a number of media personalities in these pages, but I am not going to do that. People like Al Franken and Rosie O'Donnell are soft targets; you already know what they are. No, the real villainy lies in the corporate boardrooms.

And so, let me introduce you to Jeffrey Immelt, the chief executive officer of the General Electric Corporation, the parent company of NBC. Before we examine Mr. Immelt's situation, I should tell you that some people think he's fine, a good manager. My opinion, however, is exactly the opposite.

A few years ago, some commentators on the MSNBC cable network began launching personal attacks on Fox News personnel, the Bush administration, and other Americans they deemed to be on the conservative side. The attacks were vicious and unprecedented. Never before had a network used such slander and defamation on a regular basis.

The reason behind this foray into the gutter was business, pure and simple: MSNBC was losing big in the ratings to Fox News and CNN. Simply put, the network's performance was embarrassing to NBC News and big daddy General Electric. For years MSNBC had tried to develop successful programming and had failed every single time. Eventually, their partner, Microsoft (the MS part), walked away from the disaster. That's when MSNBC decided to go into the hate business. You've heard a million times that "sex sells"; well, so does rank hatred. Maybe even more so.

Presiding over the sewer was Jeff Zucker, the head of programming at NBC. Throughout the television business, Zucker is well known as a corporate hatchet man, but in reality, he has little power. His boss can shut him down in a heartbeat. His boss is Jeffrey Immelt.

Because of the startling situation at MSNBC, I decided to take a hard look at Immelt, the big man on campus. And what I found out is extremely interesting, to say the least.

In 2001, Jeffrey Immelt took over as boss of General Electric from the legendary Jack Welch, who retired. A good soldier, with all that term implies, Immelt had been with the company since 1982 in a variety of jobs, including overseeing the "plastics" operation. I note this because of the great scene in the film *The Graduate,* when some pompous businessman urges Dustin Hoffman to seek a career in "plastics." Hoffman's dazed response is classic. Evidently, Immelt took the advice a bit more seriously.

Anyway, our man Jeff worked his way up the ladder to the top job at GE, one of America's premier companies. In April of 2002, Immelt stood before GE stockholders cheerfully promising a great future for the company. On his watch, he opined, things were going to be swell indeed. Up, up, and away, as the Fifth Dimension once sang. On the day Immelt gave his speech, the stock price for General Electric stood at about thirty-three dollars.

As I write these words, on May 26, 2008, the GE stock price is just above thirty dollars a share.

Stunningly, GE's stock price has actually *declined* about ten percent during Immelt's tenure, a ghastly performance by any measure. The millions of Americans who have held GE stock have not made a dime on their investment under Immelt's regime. And that's at a time when the overall stock market is up about thirty percent. (Remember, I can't see into the future. So anything could have happened by the time you are reading this.)

So how can something like this happen? How can Immelt, who receives about $20 million in annual compensation, still be in charge in the face of that debacle? The truth is, I don't know. And for a know-it-all like me, that is a tough admission.

But far, far worse than his awful economic performance is the fact that Jeffrey Immelt has allowed General Electric to continue doing business with Iran, one of America's most dangerous and violent enemies. For years, Immelt had to have known, since it was a matter of public record, that the Iranian government was involved in activities that directly led to thousands of American military people being killed or wounded in Iraq. Iran's bomb makers and Quds Force openly provided lethal weaponry and instruction to Iraqi terrorists. And while Americans died and suffered, Jeffrey Immelt wheeled and dealt.

In addition, Iran has publicly called for the destruction of Israel, and arms and trains terrorists to achieve that goal. An article in the *Washington Post* estimated that GE still does tens of millions of dollars' worth of business a year with the Iranian mullahs. What a disgrace.

So I sent *Factor* producer Jesse Watters to Calgary, Canada, where Immelt was speaking. Dodging security guards, Jesse asked the CEO about doing business with Iran. Incredibly, Immelt denied it on-camera. A brazen and blatant falsehood.

In fact, through subsidiaries in Italy, Canada, and France, GE has provided Iran assistance on projects including hydroelectric power, oil, and medical diagnostics. And even though Iran is currently on a list of countries that sponsor terrorism, GE doesn't seem much concerned. In a TV interview with former Disney CEO Michael Eisner *after* the *Factor* confronted him, Immelt did finally admit to doing business with Iran. Looking very concerned, ol' Jeff said that although he wanted to stop, he couldn't do it "cold turkey."

I'm sure the families who have lost soldiers and marines in Iraq understand your dilemma, right, Mr. Immelt?

I mean, how bad is this? Iran wants to murder Americans and Jews, is violating UN mandates on nuclear activity, is actively threatening the Gulf region, and Immelt can't stop doing business with them "cold turkey"?

It doesn't get much worse than that.

Despite our numerous requests to get his side of the story, Jeffrey Immelt will not speak with me. Publicly, he has stated that GE has not done anything illegal, that the U.S. government has approved his business with Iran. He also says other American companies are doing the same thing. These are excuses responsible parents wouldn't tolerate from their own kids. "It's not wrong," "someone said I could do it," and besides, "I'm stopping soon, Daddy." Even on Immelt's own terms, these are shameful excuses for helping a country that sanctions murder.

Furthermore, in a private conversation with Immelt, a high-

ranking American executive, whom I can't name because I promised him I wouldn't, asked him about the corruption at NBC News
and about GE's faltering image. "He laughed," the executive said.

Okay.

So it is my job to make sure you know all about Jeffrey Immelt
and others like him. These venal executives earn millions, are amoral
in my opinion, and act in ways that defy reason, as I understand the
term. Profit is everything to these people—even more important
than human life. The next time you use a GE lightbulb, think about
that. Think about the Iranian roadside bombs that have killed and
maimed our brave military people. Think about the thousands of
Israelis and Lebanese murdered by Hezbollah cutthroats who draw
pay from the Iranian government.

Then think about Jeffrey Immelt living in his Connecticut man-
sion, riding to work in his limo, flying in his private jet. If not me,
who's gonna call this guy out? You tell me, who is going to do it?
Brian Williams?

Sure.

Again, that kind of exposition drives me; it's what makes my
media career go. It is all about keeping accounts . . . about holding
people who harm you accountable for their actions. For sure, I'm
aware of my responsibility here. We carefully researched Jeffrey
Immelt for months before we confronted him in Canada in the fall
of 2007. Since then, *Factor* producers have called his office dozens
of times asking for explanations for his actions. But Immelt, though
an especially outrageous example of unchecked power, is just one
of many influential Americans who, I believe, are doing great damage because the system does not hold them accountable.

There is, however, acute danger in my going after bad guys. It is
twofold: First, there will be blowback; these people will come after
me. I think we've seen that repeatedly in my case. Second, there is
the potential problem of self-righteousness.

As history amply demonstrates, some crusaders for justice lose it. They become fanatics, zealots, crazed with purpose. Ralph Nader might be a good example of this. Once a great researcher and exposer of corporate corruption, Nader now sounds like Fidel Castro when he gives a speech. Corporations are evil; all politicians are in the tank! Only Ralph can save us. When he says Senators Obama and Clinton are not liberal enough, you know Ralph has left the building.

Believe me, I do think about the Nader factor when evaluating my own attitudes. I don't want to skip down the Yellow Brick Road with Ralph on the way to see the Wizard of Oz. I already have a brain, a heart, and a dose of courage. It is vital that I stay grounded in reality, fighting the fights that truly matter. I fully understand the danger of losing perspective, of seeing evildoers hiding in my closet. Luckily, I believe I've developed a fail-safe way of keeping a realistic outlook and not becoming a dragon-slaying loon.

My magic potion in this regard is free and readily available. On the label are two words: old friends.

11

MEN OF ADVENTURE

You'll be lucky if you make five good friends in your
whole life.

—WILLIAM O'REILLY SR.

My father said that to me around the time I was entering high school. Of course, I thought he was crazy. (That was my job, at the time.) After all, I had dozens of friends; just look out the window! But I never forgot my dad's statement.

Friends have always been important to me. Early on, for some reason I can't really explain, I realized the value of loyalty, shared experiences, and camaraderie. In the old neighborhood, it was the bold, fresh guy who organized the dopey games and the ridiculous nighttime raids. Over the years, it's been your humble correspondent who's kept the gang together.

Beginning in 1978, I've been organizing trips every couple of years for the "guys." My guys. My friends. The first one was to the Club Med in Playa Blanca, Mexico, and involved four of us: Joe Spencer, Jeff Cohen (of painting fame), Lou Spoto, and me.

The purpose of these trips was to cut loose and spend time.

Over time, these biannual trips have grown huge. Now as many as twenty-five guys show up to float through the Grand Canyon, explore Hawaii's Na Pali coast, or dive the waters in the British Virgin Islands. Over the past thirty years, we've had fifteen grand adventures. And every one of them contained laughs that would make Robin Williams envious.

In my younger, single days, Club Med was a prime destination for these "Men of Adventure" trips, because, at those resorts, there were plenty of women of adventure, if you know what I mean. Our needs back then were fairly basic.

If you haven't been to a Club Med, let me set the scene. It's a French-run operation that caters to young Americans looking for action. The clubs are pretty straightforward: small rooms, a nice beach or skiing mountain, and all the food you can eat. Every evening the employees put on some kind of show, but it's nothing compared to the show some of the guests participate in every day.

In the late seventies and early eighties, Club Med was at its peak. Those were the "disco years," when social mores were, well, relaxed. And Club Med sold that. The structure went like this: Club Med employees called GOs (Gentle Organizers) supervised activities, and the guests, called GMs (Gentle Members), could take them or leave them. The head of the resort, who oversaw the proceedings, was known as the Chief of the Village. Most of the employees were underpaid young Frenchmen who were allowed to romp around in the sun and pick up as many girls as they could. In fact, the employees competed with the male guests in this department, which sometimes led to some interesting situations.

One year ten Men of Adventure chaps arrived at the Club Med in Cancún, on the east coast of Mexico. Beautiful place: white sand beach, great pool, open-air hospitality. But to say the club was a zoo is to underestimate wildlife to a large degree. This resort was smoking.

The Men of Adventure, however, had a strict code, and that was

The Men of Adventure with one of Club Med's group organizers.

to play it cool under the hot Mexican sun. Many Club Med guests go wild in the first twenty-four hours of their liberation from social convention, making complete fools of themselves in the process. We would have none of *that*.

No, our rule was to stick together and not hit on any females for at least thirty-six hours into the vacation. In that way, we would present a stark contrast to all the other guys, many of whom were acting like Steve Martin and Dan Aykroyd, the wild and crazy guys of *Saturday Night Live*.

The strategy was brilliant; trust me. By day two, some of the ladies were so turned off by the zoo crew that they became curious about the "group" of men who were actually behaving like human beings (kind of).

Of course, that was a complete ruse.

Thus, on day three, when a Man of Adventure made a polite overture to a guest of the female persuasion, often said overtures were well received. It didn't take long for our social circle to rapidly expand.

Above all on these vacations, laughs were required. Very few of us got drunk; instead, we made fun of those who did. You won't be surprised to learn that much of our collective wit was directed at the rather arrogant French GOs, each of whom was given a nickname. At Cancún, for example, there was Donny Osmond, along with Lenny and Squiggy, as well as Jacques Plante (hockey goalie). Immature? You bet.

Also, we quickly discovered that many of the GOs didn't like to get wet, even though they were laboring (such as it was) at a beach resort. What they did like to do was preen in front of the ladies wearing tiny Band-Aid bathing trunks. To quote the late singer Warren Zevon singing "Werewolves of London," his "hair was perfect."

But not for long.

Acting entirely inappropriately, the Men of Adventure made it a point to actually push some of the GOs into the pool. Again, amazingly immature, simply no excuse for behaving that way. Whenever we saw a Frenchman standing at the pool's edge, we'd walk over and gently shove him into the water. Of course, everyone would laugh, including the GO, who had to play along because of guest protocol. But by midweek, they hated us, and who could blame them?

That's when I made my move.

The Games People Play

The Chief of the Village, standing about five feet five inches tall with close-cropped jet-black hair, kept a ready smile plastered on his face in public. After all, his job was to be all things to all people, all the while making sure no homicides occurred on the grounds. The guy was slick and professional, perfect for the task. I admired that.

At our initial informational resort gathering that week, the Chief told his new guests that the Cancún club had the best water polo team in all of Club Med–dom; his guys were extraordinary players, just in case we wanted to find out.

Okay.

So, my competitive appetite whetted, I planned my course of action. At lunch on day four, I approached the Chief of the Village and boldly challenged him to a water polo match: my guys against his, mano a mano. A case of champagne was riding on the outcome.

Now, *El Jefe* was no fool and realized he was staring at ten ruffians who were not buying into his program. It's not that we were disruptive; we weren't. We just couldn't help mocking the whole deal. While some other guests went "native," even trying to look like the pseudo-suave Club Med people, we remained true to our obnoxious selves. Believe me, a New York or New England edge does not easily smooth out—even in the soft breezes of the Yucatán.

But the Chief had no choice; he had to play ball (or water polo), because the challenge was made in public and the whole club was jazzed. Smiling like a madman, but blinking nonstop, the Chief of the Village accepted the deal.

The resort pool was large but shallow, so the polo match was not a test of swimming prowess; rather, it was a test of raw strength. Cleverly, the Chief insisted that both teams have at least three women to go along with seven men. There were a few amazons working at the Cancún club, and the Chief knew I couldn't match them with female guests, many of whom had never touched chlorine.

But he didn't know about the Hanson brothers.

You may remember that in 1977, Paul Newman starred in a zany film called *Slap Shot,* which chronicled the chaotic season of a minor-league ice hockcy team. Playing for Newman's squad were two brothers who were completely insane: the Hanson boys. They looked like geeks, but when the puck hit the ice, they annihilated the opposition using a variety of illegal techniques that would have frightened off the Viet Cong. Predictably, I loved those guys.

Fast-forward to the bar at Club Med Cancún. Two guys are standing at the bar. They look like brothers. They are giants, maybe six-foot-eight. They are not friendly.

Now, I had ignored these guys up until water polo challenge time. I mean, why would I intrude on their brooding time when there were twenty smiling, great-looking ladies also standing at the bar? Come on.

But after the Chief and I hammered out the water polo rules, I approached the behemoths.

"Where you guys from?" I asked matter-of-factly.

"Sacramento," one of them answered.

"Like this place?" I asked.

"Why not?" the other said.

At this point, I realized the interview was going to be short. I'm a trained professional, you know.

"You guys play ball?"

"Some."

"What sport?"

"Jim plays hoops; I play football."

"Yeah, where?"

"UC-Davis." That's the University of California at Davis, for those of you who don't watch ESPN.

"So, you want to get some exercise?" I pressed on.

"Just relaxin', man." The guys were getting bored with the conversation, so I deftly cut to the chase.

"Well, we got a water polo match against the GOs tomorrow. Want in?"

The brothers looked at each other, and Jim said, "Why not?"

Okay.

So, now I had these two giant guys, along with seven Men of Adventure thugs. (Three of the gang wouldn't play a sport if their mothers' lives depended on it, so they were sideline warriors.) Per the rules, I had to get three girls to fill out the roster.

Wasn't hard. Three of the real men had already formed "relation-ships," so their new sweeties volunteered to play as long as they didn't actually have to touch the ball. We sealed the deal.

At match time, I set my lineup. The bold, fresh guy was in the goal, because I could block just about anything and throw the ball the length of the pool with ease. Not bragging, just reporting.

The Hanson brothers were stationed at midpool. Their charge was to catch the outlet passes from me and then feed the ball to the guys close to the opposing goal. They were also under orders not to allow any French guy to run by them carrying the ball. The Hansons warmed to that assignment.

Now, I could bore you with describing in detail the bloodbath that followed, but let me keep it pithy: the Men of Adventure won the match 12–4, and the only reason the GOs scored at all was that the Hanson brothers and I left the pool with about ten minutes remain-ing in the match. We did this to bask in the adulation of the many women who attended the spectacle.

When I think back, it was gruesome. The brothers intimidated the French guys so badly that they began yelling at one another.

"Henri, you fool, pass the ball to me. . . ."

"Jacques, you clown . . ."

There was also lots of stuff in French that I didn't understand.

For added color, one of my guys, Joe Spencer, began pulling down the bathing suits of the French guys, much to the delight of the crowd. Spencer, who was six-four, about two twenty-five, wasn't the greatest athlete, but he definitely impacted the match.

Directing the proceedings from in front of the goal net, I made sure every guy on my team scored, even Lou Spoto, who did not exactly make the water polo team when he attended Harvard. In fact, he was banned from coming within a hundred yards of the pool.

That evening, the victory celebration at dinner was wild. I ac-cepted the case of champagne from the Chief of the Village and made him pose for a series of embarrassing photos. Then the Men of Adventure treated the whole place to unlimited champagne as the deejay was forced to play the Bee Gees' "Stayin' Alive."

But by far the best part of the evening was looking over at the GO table and watching those guys continue to yell at one another. Sublime.

What's in It for Me?

Now, that story is just one of thousands from my life that would all vividly back up the statement that I made at the end of the previous chapter: having old friends in your life provides a person with indelible memories, and also allows connections with the past to remain in the present.

Therefore, if I were ever to change my style, if my success or mission in life were to cause a fundamental difference in my behavior, these guys would immediately pick up on it and, believe me, let me know about it in extremely provocative ways, if you get my gist.

Over the years, I've been lucky enough to call dozens of people friends. Of course, there are varying degrees of friendship, as some folks are closer to me than others. But all the people with whom I associate are honest and speak their minds openly. No weasels among the Men of Adventure, no phonies anywhere nearby. I could never have an association with a user or sycophant, and there are strict rules of behavior for the Men and Women of Adventure. Yes, I do have women friends as well, ladies I've known forever. They are far too classy to come on the trips, but I speak with them often, and they provide yet another perspective if I get out of line.

We don't need no stinkin' Club Med!

Now, about those strict rules of kinship. What I've learned over the years is that friendship is a two-way deal, and it's not easy. People get married, have kids, get sick, lose jobs, live life. And to keep a friend through all of that, you have to be accessible. Some of my friends check in regularly, some just once in a while. But I have to know that they are there if I need them. Because they know the converse is true.

Like everybody else, I've lost friends along the way. That is inevitable, and I don't dwell on it. If somebody vanishes, I'll try to find out why. But I won't try too hard.

That's because true friendship is a choice you make. Both parties have to buy in on an equal basis. If you have to convince someone to be your friend, the concept of friendship falls apart. Like love, you can't force it.

That's why my father said you're lucky to have five friends in your entire life. He had a few friends, but not many. My mother had far more, because she was outgoing and accessible, while my father was intense and often exhausted.

Sadly, I see the concept of friendship, as I have outlined it, declining in America. With people moving around so much, the small-town neighborhood culture we once had in this country is being replaced by high-tech anonymous "friendship" that's offered on the Internet. This trend will likely weaken the social fabric of the United States, as long-term friendships, like long-term marriages, are a societal stabilizer.

For me, old friends have made me stronger and happier. In my early years, I had no idea that I would rise so high in my career; nor did my friends. They were betting on the penitentiary. But we didn't base our friendships on the expectation of material success. Some of these guys have been with me in Levittown, at St. Brigid's, through high school and college, at my first journalism job in Scranton, Pennsylvania, and onward through the decades. Never did it matter what my job was or where I lived or how much money I made. It's always been, and still is, about shared experiences and loyalty.

As you know, there are folks who form "friendships" based solely upon calculation. For example, they associate with people who can help them financially or in other material ways. That kind of cynicism is apparently acceptable in our "networking" culture. That shallow strategy, of course, leads nowhere, and people who assemble friends of convenience will wind up emotionally empty and lonely. Count on it.

Summing up, friends don't let friends forget where they came from. Should be a commercial.

Joe Spencer

On January 21, 1986, I was driving west on Route 9 in Boston, heading to my job as a reporter for WCVB-TV. As usual, I was listening to news radio when a story came on: ABC News correspondent Joe Spencer was missing in Minnesota. He'd been riding in a helicopter to cover a labor strike, and the chopper had disappeared in a severe ice storm.

Joe Spencer was my close friend.

Shaken, I pulled my car over to the side of the road and stared out the window. I prayed that Joe would be found alive. I became angry—why would a pilot risk bad weather? Then I latched on to some hope: others had survived this kind of thing in the past.

A few hours later, I learned my prayers had not been answered: no one survived the crash. Joe Spencer was thirty-two years old and newly married when he died that day.

Even now it is hard for me to write about Joseph. We met in the fall of 1977, when we were both working at KMGH-TV, the CBS-affiliated station in Denver, Colorado. We hit it off immediately: two wise guys from New York State living the single life in a vibrant city. Plus, we were both ambitious; we both were going to the top in the TV news business. If ever there were two compatible guys, we were that duo.

Personality-wise, however, we were very different. Joseph was a smooth operator and very smart, having graduated magna cum laude from Emerson College in Boston. With dark hair, piercing eyes, and a Clark Gable–style mustache, Spencer had an Italian charm that made Tony Danza look morose. The ladies loved him.

Spencer could also be calculating, but he did it with a wink. Unlike your humble correspondent, who often seeks confrontation when it is neither wise nor necessary, Spencer was a master diplomat. One

With the legendary Joe Spencer in Denver.

of the running gags between us was that, after I had rudely offended someone, Spencer would say: "What Bill really means to say is . . ."

Among my friends, the Spencer stories are legion, and thank God we had different taste in women. There was never competition in that area. He went for exotic-looking ladies; I tended to like the all-American types. In Denver, one of his frequent dates was a young Japanese woman who looked a bit like Yoko Ono. When I tactlessly questioned the attraction, Spencer simply said three words: "two-hour massage."

Okay.

What really solidified our friendship was a shared skepticism of authority and a love of adventure. At KMGH, we were both hired by a news director named Paul Thompson, an older guy who realized that, in order to get out of a deep ratings slump, the station needed energy and daring. Thompson encouraged Spencer and me to aggressively report wrongdoing, and we did. Soon, Spencer and O'Reilly became very popular in Colorado. And then Paul Thompson left the station.

He was replaced by the devil. We saw the moving-van receipts from hell.

Both Spencer and I immediately despised the new guy, because he didn't like us and, we thought, probably didn't like baby seals, either. There are many reasons not to like me, but Spencer was another story; most human beings found him engaging. Not the devil, however; he disliked Spencer more than me, which is some kind of perversion, let me tell you.

Looking back, the new boss was probably trying to send a signal that two young hotshots were not going to run him around. He would *show* them.

Sure.

As with many TV stations, KMGH paid outside media consultants to tell them how to present the news. Every few months, these hired assassins would ride into town and inform station management who should be fired and who should be hired. In fact, I actually got my job in Denver because a consultant saw me in Dallas, where I was working, and suggested Paul Thompson sign me up.

Anyway, both Spencer and I had always done well with consultants, because we were pretty good reporters and performed well on air. But the new boss had some bad news for both of us: according to the latest consultant report, we were terrible. Awful. A complete disgrace. We had to improve or else.

Okay.

Neither Spencer nor I believed this guy, because, as stated, he was the devil, and who in his right mind would believe Lucifer? So we quickly came to the conclusion that he was messing with us. Of course, that could not stand. So we hatched a plan.

KMGH is located on Speer Boulevard, a short distance from downtown Denver. At night, the station hired a watchman, but he usually slept in the lobby. The newsroom was located on the second floor, and by midnight, it was usually deserted.

One Saturday night, after some late-night disco carousing at the

London House club, Spencer and I decided to break into the news
director's office with the hope of finding the consultant's report. We
wanted to see the research for ourselves. Of course, this was insane,
a crime. We were breaking and entering. We went ahead anyway.

After a few hours of "socializing," Spencer was a bit buzzed, but
I was clear-eyed and determined. We would be like the Watergate
break-in guys, but we would not get caught. We were agile, quick
like cats. We were also stupid.

The first problem was access. The primary way to enter the station was through the lobby, but the dozing watchman eliminated
that route. There was, however, a locked door on the east side of
the building. Spencer was confident he could pick the lock. When I
asked why he was so sure of himself, he answered with two words:
"I'm Sicilian." (His family name was Spalletta.)

Check.

Now, I have trouble unlocking a door from the *inside,* but Spencer smoothly inserted his credit card, moved it around a bit, and the
lock sprang open. What a guy.

We then crept quietly up the stairs and walked into the dark-
ened newsroom, where Satan's glass-enclosed office took up space
against the west wall. Again, the door was locked. Again, Spencer
jimmied it open. We rifled through Lucifer's files (arranged alpha-
betically) and quickly located the consultant's folder. There in front
of us were the staff evaluations. Both Spencer and I were considered "valued employees." The devil had deceived us.

Okay.

So now we had to decide what to do. Of course, we couldn't
go around quoting the consultant's report, because that would raise
many questions and perhaps lead to a dusting for fingerprints. Then
I, the bold, fresh guy, actually came up with a strategy that didn't
even involve kneecapping the news director.

No, both Spencer and I would go to see the general manager of
the station and offer our resignations.

At first, Spencer was aghast. That might be a little too much "adventure," even for him. But when I explained the beauty of my plan, he quickly wised up. Listen to this scheme and tell me it isn't brilliant.

We would go see the station general manager, Bob Hart, who generally liked us. We would tell him—very humbly, of course—that the news director had informed us that our work was poor. Because of that, in good conscience, we could no longer take the station's money. Our honor would not permit it. We'd have to resign.

Was this brilliant or what? The problem was the humble part. I could not fake that, but Spencer could, so he would have to do the talking. Which he did. His performance was so nuanced that Robert De Niro would have taken notes. Of course, we knew that Hart had almost certainly seen the consultant's report (since he paid for it) and would immediately understand that Satan had lied to us.

I'll never forget the stoic look on Bob Hart's face when he said, "Don't worry about it, guys; you're doing fine."

Beelzebub was never the same after that. He left me and Spencer completely alone, and months later, he was fired. Chalk one up for God.

Over the eight years of our friendship, Joe Spencer and I traveled the world together and helped each other climb the TV ladder. After two years of working in Denver, I left to take an anchor job in Hartford, Connecticut. A few months after that, I got lucky and was hired by WCBS-TV in New York City.

Spencer followed me out of the Mile High City, taking a job in Detroit at WXYZ-TV. There, he kicked some serious butt and went on to take a correspondent's job in the Chicago bureau of ABC News.

It was while he was on assignment for ABC's *Good Morning America* that his chopper went down.

As I said, part of my reaction to Joe Spencer's death was anger. That's how I sometimes cope with things completely out of my control. I was furious that my friend was gone, leaving a young, brokenhearted wife as well as a grief-stricken mother, father, and brother. It was all so senseless.

Three days after he died, Joe Spencer's funeral was held in his hometown, Amsterdam, New York. I was to give the eulogy. I didn't want to do it. For once in my life, I didn't know what to say.

Also speaking that day was ABC News anchorman Peter Jennings. I had met him a couple of times but didn't really know him. Neither did Spencer. Because he was based in Chicago, Spencer had had little interaction with the powerful Jennings, who lived in New York City.

Keep in mind that on the day of the funeral, anger was still raging inside me. I arrived at the church not wanting any BS. I knew Jennings had prepared some remarks, and I had some reservations about that. So I took him aside in the sacristy, and the conversation went something like this:

O'Reilly: Mr. Jennings, thanks for coming; the family appreciates it. Can you tell me what you're going to say?

Jennings (looking a bit surprised): I thought I'd concentrate on Joe's value to ABC News, his abilities.

O'Reilly: Good. Because we both realize that you didn't know him very well, so I don't think you should get into the personal stuff too much. Let me handle that.

Jennings (his eyebrows raised a bit): Fine. I think that's right. You handle the personal; I'll talk about what he meant to ABC.

O'Reilly: Good. Appreciate it.

The priest, standing by, overheard the conversation. When Jennings left the sacristy, he said, "Well, that took guts."

"Not really, Father," I replied. "It's just such a terrible thing. I want it done the right way."

"Are you all right?" he asked.

"I'm angry. It won't show."

"Go easy on yourself, son."

"Yeah."

A few minutes later, I walked up to the altar and told the packed church that Joe Spencer lived more in thirty-two years than most people do in eighty. I told them that he was a unique force, an unusually generous and loving guy. I told them about his sense of justice and his sense of mischief. I wrote down nothing. The words just came.

Those were some of the worst days of my life. A few months later, ABC News offered me a correspondent's job, partly, I believe, because Peter Jennings saw something in me that he liked and perhaps respected.

In fact, I took the job because of Jennings. Think about it: he could have been offended that some nobody was telling him what to say at a funeral. He could have been like that. But he wasn't.

Up until he died in 2005, I kept in touch with Peter. I respected him immensely. He "got" Joe Spencer, and he "got" me. Furthermore, after working with him, I came to understand his compassion and intellect. Both Joe and Peter were great men.

You should know that I actually did not want to write the story I just told you. I deliberated a long time before deciding to tell it. My friendship with Joe Spencer was so personal that I rarely speak about it. But, as with my other friends, he enriched my life and greatly contributed to my success.

So now everybody knows, Joe.

Full Circle

One of the best things I've ever done didn't make the papers or cause an uproar on national television. On June 18, 1988, I put together

a reunion for my St. Brigid's School classmates, simply because I
wanted to see those people again. Of the fifty-five kids who graduated in June 1963, thirty-five showed up to celebrate old friendships
in a restaurant a couple of blocks away from our old school. It had
been exactly twenty-five years since we were all in the same room.

On that warm, cloudy Northeastern evening, goodwill and great
humor swirled in the air. There was no awkwardness or pretension
at all; everybody just naturally started hugging and laughing. It was
a great night. Here's what I wrote about it a few weeks later:

Twenty-five years is an unthinkable amount of time when
you are a child. But it has passed, and the sight of my
former St. Brigid's classmates back together again was both
disconcerting and exhilarating.

I had not been called Billy since I left St. Brigid's, but I was
Billy again and, somehow, it sounded right. My former classmates,
all approaching forty years old, seemed the same to me.

Marybeth, always the perfect teacher's pet, still seemed
perfect as she worked the room with warmth and charm.
Anne Marie had remained sweet and shy. She remembered
everything, down to the lessons in our *Think-and-Do Book*s.
JC, always adventurous, showed up sporting an earring and
pirate sideburns. No one was surprised.

Most of the class had stayed on Long Island. Because of
family, many said. All the women had married except for
one. Most had kids. Most of the men had families as
well. Almost everyone was middle-class, and, somewhat
surprisingly, the majority of the class had stayed with the
Catholic Church.

The memories were fabulous. Sister Thomas making
Barbara put the gum she was chewing on her nose, the
entire class creating chaos at the theater showing *The
Song of Bernadette*. Everybody remembering Clement's

I still get together with many of my old friends for such occasions as this rafting trip down the Colorado River.

hilarious exploits. Many were shocked when they heard he had died.

We all raised a toast to Clem, for he had provided us with a spirit of mischief and individuality that every child should have. And then we toasted one another. Although we would perhaps never be physically together again, we would always be emotionally attached. We had grown up side by side, overcoming fears, forming consciences, and learning how to live.

The reunion got to me, and I am not a sentimental man. But interacting once again with my childhood classmates filled in some important blanks in my life.

My classmates and I learned many lessons in our eight years together, but, for me, the most important lesson was realized only after we reunited. Looking at the happy faces, hearing the laughter and sharing the memories, it was clear that we all had absorbed something that simply cannot be taught; we had learned the value of one another.

For me, that description *is* a bit sentimental. But I didn't know how else to write it.

There are a number of on-ramps to memory lane, but, for me, the experiences important to shaping my life are all tied into how I behave today. The opinions I dish out, the actions I take, even the thoughts I think, are all guided by my belief system, which, as you've read, was forged in childhood. I am proud of that legacy; it has served me well.

While researching this book, I came across my eighth-grade autograph book: you know, the one where your classmates wish you good luck, tell dumb jokes, and such.

One entry stands out. Written on the very last page—actually, on the book's cardboard back frame—are these words:

> To Bill
>> If anybody wishes you more Luck than me
>> Let him sign his name after me
>>> Good Luck Always,
>>> Clem

SLUGGING IT OUT

My buddies and me,
Are getting real well known,
Yeah, the bad guys know us,
And they leave us alone.

— THE BEACH BOYS, "I GET AROUND"

Sometimes I wonder what my father would think of my success. Some of you may have the same feeling. When my father was dying of cancer in August 1985, he knew I had succeeded as a TV reporter in New York, but, of course, he had no idea of what was to come. I was still on the march. I had not yet reached my cruising altitude. My greatest success lay more than a decade away.

Based upon his conversations, my father seemed to admire my grit and earning prowess. Typically, when I visited home, he would say, "Do you realize that you're making more money than anybody in this neighborhood?"

Truthfully, I really didn't care, because economic success has never been a priority for me. But my father cared a lot, because

money, to a Depression survivor like him, had implications far beyond purchasing power. Cash assets signified victory over the spec-
ter of calamity. But, most important, it brought closer to home the
greatest word in the English language: security.

Last year, I was able to donate more money to charity than my
father had earned in his entire lifetime. How would he have processed that? I simply don't know. William O'Reilly Sr. never even
knew a rich person, not one. How would he have looked upon his
now-wealthy son?

I can tell you this: my father's relationship with currency made
a deep impression on me, but in a rather unusual way. He taught
frugality; I learned the lesson. He mocked materialists; so do I. He
would actually suffer to save money; I draw the line right there.

In the spring of 1965, when I was fifteen years old, the O'Reilly
family made a rare out-of-state vacation trip to sunny Fort Lauderdale, Florida. Gidget, here I come, right? Well, not exactly. About
the only way I would have spied the G-girl or any other lovely young
damsel was if she had been sitting on the grimy Greyhound bus we
rode down to the Sunshine State.

If you've never taken a thirty-hour bus ride, stopping only at dank
terminals to pick up a variety of wanted felons, I have just one word
for you: DON'T. Dante had no idea. That was *really* hell.

I'll keep my description brief. The New Jersey Turnpike smelled
pretty bad as we rode along, but nothing like the inside of that bus
once we passed Richmond, Virginia, around hour ten. Food came
from the bus terminals. My father ate it; my mother, sister, and I did
not. Passengers ranged from drunk to incoherent to mumbling stuff
no young man should ever hear. For the first time in her entire life
my sister, Janet, then age thirteen, actually hissed at my father when
he asked her how she was doing.

My mother's rosary beads got a heavy workout.

Finally, we rolled into Fort Lauderdale for five exciting days and nights. Followed by, of course, another excruciating bus ride home. Are you getting the O'Reilly family vacation picture? Good.

The Spartan life we led back then has stayed with me to this day. I spend money on important things, like living space, good food, and security. I travel first-class, no buses ever. I get a stomachache just looking at a bus.

Also, I don't waste money on stupid stuff like vanity possessions. So my father taught me well, at least in areas not involving public transportation.

When I entered the workforce after graduating from college, my dad told me that his job was done; he had provided for my education, and now I had to prove myself in the real world. It wasn't a callous statement, just a definition of where we stood. There would be no living subsidies, no gifts of the automotive variety. I was on my own.

Now, as I've outlined, I wasn't very dependent on my parents in the first place. I rarely went to them for advice; I never asked them for money. Whenever I read about family dynasties like the Kennedys and the Bushes, I'm fascinated and maybe, in my subconscious, a bit jealous. I don't think so, but anything is possible.

While many parents these days micromanage their children or shuttle them off to nannies or day-care providers, my folks were just the opposite. My father had no clue what my future would be and, truthfully, avoided much conversation about it. He and my mother cared, but from a distance. Through the years, whenever I whined about some workplace injustice, my father's reply always met his usual pithy and snappy standards: "Slug it out."

Okay.

This will not come as a shock to you, but to say I went to work with a chip on my shoulder is like saying Britney Spears might have made a few bad decisions—stating the obvious. But here's the beauty of being the bold, fresh guy in the world of journalism:

that edge made me work harder than most everybody else in the newsroom. I'd get that damn story no matter what. If somebody tried to con me with an evasive answer, I'd confront that person immediately. I was a one-person walking "no-spin zone" long before I thought up the description.

Thus, I moved up fast: Nine months in Scranton, Pennsylvania, then a jump to the major market of Dallas–Fort Worth. Two years later, I took a weekend anchor job in Denver. Then I was hired as a primary anchor in Hartford, Connecticut. Finally, after only five years in the TV news business, I was back home in New York City, anchoring a newsmagazine program on big gun WCBS-TV.

My father, of course, had no idea how all of that happened and never really asked. Suddenly, there I was on his TV set, and that was fine with him.

My mother didn't really ask about my career, either. That's because pretty much anything I did was okay with her. Both my parents watched me on the tube and accepted the congratulations of some stunned neighbors, but my media job was never a big deal to them.

One of my assignments took me to El Salvador, where things were a bit dangerous. In the early 1980s, the government there was slugging it out with some communist insurgents, and the conflict was brutal. After a harrowing day in the war zone, I called my parents from the InterContinental Real San Salvador Hotel, where the CBS crew was based. My mother answered the phone.

"Mom, hey, how are you?"

"Fine, dear. Where are you?"

"El Salvador."

"Oh. Here's your father."

"Where are you?"

"El Salvador, Dad."

"What are you doing there?"

"Covering the war."

"Are you paying for this call?"

"CBS pays, Dad."

"Well, I don't want to run up the tab. Need anything?"

"No, I'm fine."

"What's it like there?"

"Pretty intense."

"Well, you take care."

"See you, Dad."

Now, some people might find that exchange on the strange side, but to me it was perfectly normal. My parents simply *had no idea*. They had no reference point for a discussion. El Salvador? Covering a war? They had no idea what was involved and assumed I'd be fine, because I'd always fended for myself without much drama (as far as they knew).

There was also their shared discomfort with any "worry factor." My father did not want to dwell on my problems or those of anyone else. He had enough stuff on his plate. For him, disaster was always looming someplace (that Depression mentality again), and to take on my potential disappointments was just too much. Despite my bold, fresh status, I somehow completely understood this at a very early age.

On the other hand, my mother prayed for my sister and me with complete faith that God would protect us. My mom and God are quite close. Again, I understood and accepted my mother's view on life. Her fears (mainly of accidents and illnesses) were quite different from my father's, but they influenced everything she did. Since there was no way that I could do anything about the demons that my parents fought, I simply accepted the home-front situation and was a lot stronger for doing that. Few expectations meant few disappointments. Some family situations are soap operas. Not in my case.

Admittedly, the lack of a vocational support system or wise counsel when things got difficult put me at a disadvantage in the marketplace. No question about that. But I got very good at "slugging it out."

And I needed that skill, because, to this day, I have to deal with some very bad people in TV land. Most of the time, I defeat them. Most of the time.

One quick story that will illuminate my attitude toward bad behavior, my crusader mentality that often makes my TV program hum. After leaving CBS on bad terms at the end of 1982 (the intense story is chronicled in my novel, *Those Who Trespass*), I was reunited with my old WCBS boss, Jeff Schiffman, in Boston. Jeff was second in command at WNEV-TV (now WHDH-TV) and had very kindly secured a well-paying weekend anchor job for the bold, fresh guy. One big problem: Schiffman wasn't my direct supervisor; a guy named Bill Applegate was.

And Applegate was *not* a fan of the bold, fresh approach.

In early 1983, WNEV was like Saigon right before the fall of Vietnam: chaos everywhere. Applegate had hired a bunch of cruel, crude managers who terrorized the news staff using gestapo-like tactics of fear and intimidation. I mean, it was brutal: good people were publicly humiliated, and more than a few were fired on the spot, security goons quickly escorting them from the building. Ask any veteran of the Boston media: they'll back me up when I tell you that WNEV-TV was the Little Big Horn of local TV news.

The big problem was ratings. They were awful. They had always been terrible, but now Applegate, despite being given millions to spend, was making them worse. The primary problem was that our competitors, WBZ-TV and WCVB-TV, employed legendary New England anchors like Jack Williams and Natalie Jacobson. They were loved in that market. So WNEV was up against it from the jump.

No matter, the bold, fresh guy did his job and, as always, worked hard. Initially, Applegate's sadists pretty much left me alone, but every day I would see those pinheads brutalizing my coworkers. And every day I would get angrier.

Finally, the shoe dropped. I was typing up a script for air when one of the SS brigade approached. He was about thirty-five years old, short, balding, with a flat Midwestern accent.

"O'Reilly, what are you doing tomorrow?"

"Probably coming to work; it's Wednesday."

"Yeah, well, when you get here, I want you to have two stories set up." (That meant that this clown expected me to have what are called "enterprise" stories ready to shoot. Those are usually feature reports about subjects of interest that are unique in some way. One enterprise piece is difficult to develop that quickly, two nearly impossible.)

"Sure," I said flippantly. "Check with me tomorrow."

The man's voice got louder: "What was that?"

Somewhere in my subconscious mind, I believe a vision of the Chaminade clip-on-tie incident kicked in, because I was boiling fast. Folks in the newsroom looked up; typing stopped. A quiet moment in time fell on the bustling floor.

Slowly, for optimum effect, I arose from my chair. The clown was standing to my left, and I stepped close to him. Clenching my jaw (no effect here; I was angry), I looked into his beady brown eyes and growled, "I said, 'Check with me tomorrow.'"

His eyeballs darted back and forth in a Sister Thomas–like movement. He licked his lips.

"Don't talk to *me* like that."

In a flash, I grabbed the guy's tie and pulled it tight around his neck. Holding on firmly, I dragged him across the newsroom and into assistant news director Jim Johnson's office. I closed the door. Hard.

"Jim, if this guy talks to me again, I'll break his nose."

"O'Reilly, calm down. You can't threaten a manager."

"One more time, Jim, he's in the emergency room. And I'm calling the union rep right now. This idiot is out of line."

Now, the interesting thing is that, throughout all of this, the guy I was threatening said nothing. He just stood there with a stupid look on his face. Johnson, a good guy, didn't even address him. Jim knew what was going on in the newsroom but was in a tough spot. He was powerless to change the station's management style, even though he knew it was wrong. Now a minicrisis had blown into his office.

Obviously, the bold, fresh guy had challenged management in front of everybody. Mutiny was brewing anyway, and if this got out of control, lifeboats might hit the water. Judging from his twitching facial muscles, Johnson was thinking fast.

"I want you to calm down, Bill," Johnson said in a reasonable tone.

"Fine. I'm calm. Keep him away from me." And I walked out of the office.

A short time later my friend, Jeff Schiffman, called me into his office and we talked about the situation. He told me that Applegate wanted to fire me, but since I had a guaranteed contract, Win Baker, the general manager, didn't want the bad publicity that a public exposition would cause. Schiffman told me to shut up and avoid any felonies.

A short time later, God intervened: Applegate left the station, his zombie hit men closely following him out the door.

Now, did I do the right thing? Not career-wise, that's for sure. Stories about me in the TV business are legendary. In some versions of the above, I threw the guy into Boston Harbor.

But I see it this way: I've got one life and no stomach for swallowing garbage like that. I took my chances. I slugged it out.

Do I recommend that attitude for others? No, I don't. I am damn lucky to have survived in the TV business after pulling stuff like that. But, for me, it proved to be basic training for what I am doing now on the *Factor*: taking on the villains that are hurting the country. As you may know, my team of producers is perhaps the most feared in the media. If you abuse Americans, especially children, we will hunt you down. Bad judges, corrupt politicians and media people, evildoers of all kinds are liable to be confronted at any time.

My programs are dedicated to holding dishonest and downright bad people accountable for what they do.

But far from being heralded in all quarters, this approach has caused major controversy. Who else does this on television? Who else makes judgments and exposes the powerful? Sometimes *60 Minutes,* once in a while *Frontline.* Brian Ross does a good job on ABC News. But on a daily basis, the *Factor* is it.

Those who see the world differently than I do are not happy about my work. In fact, some of them object strenuously to my very existence—and vilify me at every opportunity. That's why I have to have security people. Believe me, if I didn't have a fire within, I would never put myself at such risk.

Once again, I hope you're not reading this explanation as some kind of macho ego trip. I'm just trying to explain why I do what I do. How the *Factor* concept has become a crusade, albeit a polarizing one to some. It is my personal decision to "slug it out"; nobody encouraged me to be me. But it has worked.

Finally, my coanchor in Boston was a very pretty woman from a civilized background, nothing at all like me. After witnessing the newsroom display I just described and a bunch of other stuff like it, she would just shake her head, sigh, and tell me that I would never win with the confrontational approach.

I hope she's enjoying reading this book.

CHAPTER

13

POWER

Being powerful is like being a lady. If you have to tell people you are, you aren't.

—MARGARET THATCHER

In America, power and fame frequently intersect. A famous face opens doors, gets restaurant tables, and is offered all kinds of perks. That's power, in a sense. For example, nitwits like Paris Hilton and the rapper 50 Cent have that kind of a situation. They are certainly not powerful people, but in this celebrity-mad age, they derive benefit from their notoriety.

But the truly powerful on this earth all have one thing in common: their actions and ideas can directly affect the lives of other people. In this country, that means that you and I can be disturbed, assisted, inconvenienced, or strengthened by the powerful. In this chapter, that is the definition of power that we'll explore.

Back in Levittown, my family and I were essentially powerless. My parents had power over my sister and me, but that was it. And I had no power whatsoever, until I became a teacher at age twenty-one. Sadly, the O'Reilly clan was like many families all over the world:

completely at the mercy of outside forces. As we discussed, that is never a good thing.

Growing up, I had two minor brushes with fame. Some of you will remember the program *Ben Casey,* a medical drama that ran on ABC from 1961 to 1966. The star of the show was a brooding actor named Vince Edwards, who, each week, scrubbed up, defied authority, and healed the sick. Dr. Casey, as I remember it, was usually tecd off while treating patients, perhaps because another TV medical guy—Dr. Kildare, played by Richard Chamberlain—was getting better ratings.

Anyway, Vince Edwards's older brother actually lived on Patience Lane! He was the neighborhood celebrity. My gang, of course, nicknamed him Ben, which he did not like one bit. We, of course, could not have cared less.

One fine summer day, without warning, the famous Vince Edwards himself pulled up in a black Cadillac to visit his brother. Immediately, chaos broke out. The entire neighborhood swarmed onto Patience Lane. This was huge!

At that moment, the bold, fresh guy was playing baseball at the Caddy House field, about a half mile away from Patience Lane. Suddenly, the game was interrupted when a Paul Revere–like figure appeared on a bicycle.

"Ben Casey is at his brother's house!" the kid yelled. "He's really here!"

Not even pausing for a response, the young Revere then pedaled off to tell the rest of the world of events second only to Lexington and Concord.

That was it for the game, as most of the guys, understandably, wanted to check out Ben Casey. Mildly curious myself, I joined the bicycle exodus riding toward the action. Unfortunately, we got there too late. Little Helen Hanley, the younger sister of my friend Paul, ran over and told me that Ben Casey had just departed. Holding up a wrinkled piece of paper, she proudly displayed his autograph.

Helen was in heaven.

At dinner that night my mother told my father that Vince Edwards had visited the neighborhood. My dad finished chewing, looked up from the overcooked meat loaf, and said this: "So?"

My father was pithy long before Dick Cheney.

My other brush with fame occurred nearly a decade later and was a bit more complicated. As I mentioned, I wrote a column for the *Circle,* the Marist College student newspaper, coedited by my roommate, Joe Rubino. Because we were constantly broke, Rubino and I were constantly looking for ways to, uh, beat the capitalistic system. Yeah, that's it.

Eventually, we came up with a scheme that would allow us access to almost every entertainment and sporting event imaginable, free of charge. Feeling no remorse whatsoever, we founded a fictional press operation called the Intercollegiate Press.

Stay with me here, because this is brilliant.

Located on the eastern bank of the Hudson River, Marist College, back then, didn't have a lot of amenities. It was a basic place: three dormitories, a library, a small gym. The snooty Vassar girls who lived on the other side of town might have called the campus "quaint."

But what Marist did have was its own little printing plant run by a man who looked to be about a hundred and six years old. Nice guy, no clue. Because Rubino was constantly getting stuff legitimately printed for the *Circle,* the ancient guy would pretty much run off whatever Rubino gave him.

One day, we ordered two very official-looking press cards, each with our names clearly printed above this impressive imprint:

Intercollegiate Press
The Only Weekly News-Letter Devoted to Current College Events
Published During the Academic Year

Is that solid or what? Of course, there was no Intercollegiate Press. At least, not on this planet.

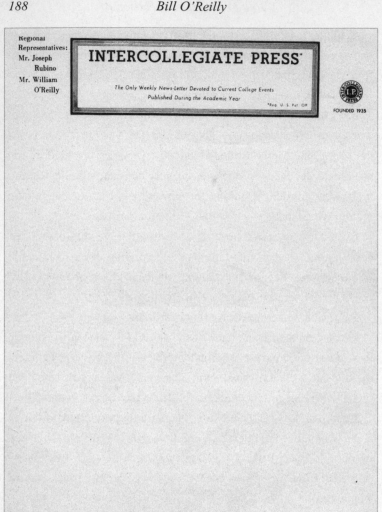

Regional
Representatives:
Mr. Joseph
    Rubino
Mr. William
    O'Reilly

INTERCOLLEGIATE PRESS˙

The Only Weekly News-Letter Devoted to Current College Events
Published During the Academic Year

*Reg. U. S. Pat. Off.

FOUNDED 1935

Our famously effective letterhead.

Credentials at the ready, Rubino then got the printer to churn out one thousand sheets of paper with the IP letterhead. Armed with the press cards and the very impressive-looking paper, we got busy.

Letters flew out of Poughkeepsie to many different concerns, and when the dust settled, we had secured free movie passes, Broadway play tickets, and complimentary admission to any ABA basketball game in the world. And listen to this: We also scored season's tickets for THE NEW YORK YANKEES! My God.

Once in a while, some public relations person would ask us what the Intercollegiate Press actually *did*. For example, where was it published? Where did the articles appear? Our reply was superslick: IP was a college wire service that went out to thousands of campus newspapers whose editors then made their own choices. Sometimes the editors incorporated the information we supplied into other articles written by their reporters; sometimes they used our writing as stand-alone stories. As they say in prison, it was all good.

Now, if Sister Lurana had known about this con, she would have collapsed on the spot. But, rationalizing like crazy, Rubino and I felt no shame. After all, who were we hurting? No one. And who were we helping? Us. Case closed.

Flush with initial success, we became more daring. In February 1971, I wrote to *The Tonight Show Starring Johnny Carson,* then produced in New York City, and requested tickets so we could do a behind-the-scenes article on Ed McMahon, his sidekick. That, of course, would be for the benefit of millions of American college students hungry to know more about Ed, with whom they all identified.

Sure.

Almost miraculously, two weeks later, a letter arrived telling us where to pick up the tickets for the March 17 broadcast.

That's right, St. Patrick's Day, the Irish display time. This was great. Back then the Carson program was enormous; the entire country loved it and him. And now we had free tickets. What a coup!

As Irish luck would have it, Rubino and the bold, fresh guy were already slated to be in the city that day, because that's where the girls would be: celebrating their favorite guy, Saint Patrick. So things were falling into place perfectly.

On game day, we drove to New York in Rubino's brown, tinny Plymouth Duster, watched a bit of the big parade on Fifth Avenue, and then wandered over to Rockefeller Center to pick up the tickets.

Tenth row, on the aisle. Choice.

However, whenever things are going too well, you know a change is due. To our utter shock and disappointment, Carson was off that night and Joey Bishop was subbing. Joey Bishop? Good grief! This was not good.

For those who don't know him, Joey Bishop was a gentle comedian best known for hanging around with Frank Sinatra and Dean Martin. For some reason that, to this day, no one can quite figure out, Bishop was a certified member of the Rat Pack, which consisted of Sammy Davis Jr. and Peter Lawford, as well as Frank and Dean. The Pack roamed around partying and cracking wise, all the while milking an enormous amount of publicity. But, believe me, Joey Bishop was a steep drop-off from Johnny Carson, like going from lobster to tuna.

Slouching insolently in our fine seats, we watched as Joey took the stage and quickly ran out of material. He then grabbed a microphone and *walked into the audience.* Rubino and I quickly straightened up as Joey sauntered up the aisle, heading directly toward *us.*

I remember thinking, Why not? So I simply arose from my seat, all six-foot-four of me, towering over Joey, who was almost a foot shorter. Rubino, about five-nine, quickly stood as well.

"What can I do for you guys?" the comedian asked warily as he approached.

"Uh, we're celebrating St. Patrick's Day and want to wish you a happy one," I said, like a moron.

Bishop smiled. "How are you celebrating?"

Thinking very slowly, I said: "We're gonna get ripped."

Joey looked bemused and said to Rubino: "How about you?"

Whereupon Rubino put forth the immortal line: "I'm Italian."

The conversation went downhill from there and ended seconds later. On page 176 of my first book, *The O'Reilly Factor,* I briefly mention that we attempted to extort a dinner from Joey before sitting down. Grim but true.

Dazed by the experience, I then sat through the show, and I swear, I can't remember another thing about it.

After leaving the studio, a jazzed Rubino immediately called Marist and spoke with his coeditor on the *Circle*. After listening to the story, the guy didn't believe that Rubino and I would be on *The Tonight Show* later that evening. Let me repeat that. HE DID NOT BELIEVE.

Instantly, I knew this was a big break. So we leaped into the Duster and drove quickly back to Poughkeepsie. Along the way, we hatched the plot.

The Tonight Show was taped at five in the afternoon, so, driving fast, we got back to Marist College around eight forty-five p.m. Our plan was to make as many cash bets as possible asserting that we would be seen and heard on NBC that very evening. Racing through the dorms, we covered about two hundred dollars in wagers from fellow students, some in various stages of intoxication.

Ignoring derisive chants from foolish skeptics, Rubino and I finished recording the bets and then forced some freshman tech expert to move a TV onto the college theater stage (no personal TVs were allowed in the rooms back then). By eleven thirty, the place was filled to capacity.

At exactly eleven thirty-five a giant roar went up from the crowd.

The next day the campus was on fire.

Some of the professors were appalled, truculently accusing Rubino and me of giving the college a bad name (we had mentioned to Joey that we were attending Marist). I replied in the *Circle* that if Professor Zucarello thought the college's name could get any worse, he was nuts.

And so it went.

Good story, right? Besides entertainment, my point for bringing it up is to demonstrate that before I got into the TV news business, I had zero experience with power brokers, and only two rather pathetic brushes with the fame game. It was only after I got into the news business that I began to understand how the American system *really* works. Power drives this country, and there are both good and bad people behind the wheel.

To me, it is simply amazing that I have traveled from Ben Casey and Joey Bishop to personally knowing many of the most powerful people in the world. Not bragging, just reporting.

So let's take a look at how things really work.

Ladies and Gentlemen, the President of the United States

Even though I firmly believe the United States is a noble nation, I also understand full well that some powerful Americans are not noble (see Jeffrey Immelt). Currently, it is my job to deal with these people and, if need be, persuade them to do the right thing. Sometimes, I'm successful in that quest. Sometimes, I'm not.

When I can't reason with powerful people who, in my view, are hurting the folks, I expose them on national TV and radio. This, of course, does not make some power brokers big fans of mine. "Who is this punk O'Reilly spouting off on cable?" they must be thinking. "How can this be happening?"

I must confess that annoying powerful bad guys is a great part of my job.

In assessing the powerful, there are many avenues to explore. The grandest boulevard, of course, is the domain of the most powerful person in the world: the President of the United States.

Your humble correspondent, the bold, fresh guy, has interacted with four presidents, and again, I always wonder what my late father would have thought about that. Remember, he had a cynicism about the powerful, and while he loved his country, he was never in awe of presidents or anyone else. So I am left wondering just how my father would have processed my access to these people.

Anyway, let's begin the power presentation with the president I know best.

Three times I have interviewed George W. Bush, and here is my assessment: I believe he is an honest man. I believe his presidency was challenged by extraordinarily difficult circumstances that only a few other chief executives have ever faced. The terror attack on September 11 instantly changed the world, introducing a complex set of unique circumstances to Americans. Understanding that, I do cut President Bush some slack, unlike many in the media.

That being said, President Bush has made some major mistakes, most of which were exacerbated by what I call "the rich-guy syndrome." Let me explain. For people like me, raised in working-class homes, disaster is always in play, constantly present on the horizon. As I mentioned, both my mother and father were possessed by a nagging fear that stuff would inevitably go wrong. This is common among everyday folks who have to work hard to get by.

But Americans born into wealth and power usually do not have that fear. That's because things always seem to work out for them. Money buys security from harm and often can mitigate difficult situations. Power, as we've discussed, leads to opportunities. You must accept that truism in order to understand President Bush and his approach to vexing problems.

The crowning achievement of the Bush administration, usually ignored by the bitter left-wing media, is the hurt it put on al Qaeda. Within a year after 9/11, President Bush and his allies had delivered a series of devastating blows to the Islamic extremist community. The Taliban were routed in Afghanistan, dozens of al Qaeda leaders and operatives around the world were captured or killed, and scores of countries cooperated with America in freezing suspected terrorist bank accounts.

President Bush was flush with success. In most polls, his approval ratings were above eighty percent.

Then came the invasion of Iraq and the unraveling of the President's initial terror war success. As you know, the "Bush lied" crowd cannot stop screaming that the President fabricated the reasons for removing the tyrant Saddam Hussein. The prevailing wisdom on the far left is that Bush is a savage warmonger intent, for venal reasons, on imposing American dominance on the world. The anti-Bush partisans paint a harsh picture, and unfortunately, many people believe it. But that analysis is largely bull.

In fact, when I interviewed former White House spokesperson Scott McClellan on the *Factor*, he couldn't back up his well-publicized book assertion that the Bush administration used "propaganda" to take the nation to war. I crushed McClellan by saying President Clinton and British Prime Minister Tony Blair had backed up Mr. Bush. They saw the same intel on Iraq that he did. Were they pushing "propaganda" as well?

McClellan looked confused.

In fact, the mantra that Bush "lied" about Iraq is itself a lie and completely absurd on its face.

No, there *was* compelling evidence that Saddam had been hoarding deadly weapons of mass destruction and could well hand them off to a variety of terrorists (Hamas, Muslim Brotherhood, etc.) whenever he chose to. Captured documents after Saddam's fall prove beyond a reasonable doubt that the dictator told his own generals he had secret caches of WMDs and was ready to use them. Many of Saddam's generals now confirm this.

On worldwide television, former CIA director George Tenet looked me in the eye and said he presented President Bush with intel that also confirmed the existence of Iraqi WMDs and other dangerous plots. Of course, the WMD intelligence turned out to be wrong, but there's a big difference between a mistake and a lie.

Nonetheless, I have to agree with critics that the post-Saddam planning by the Bush administration was abysmal. Soon after Saddam was pushed from power, I told my audience that American forces were not nearly aggressive enough in controlling the looting that was taking place in Iraq. I was amazed and depressed by the chaos. Why wasn't this kind of lawlessness anticipated?

But, apparently, President Bush was not equally appalled. Furthermore, as subsequent events spiraled downward in Iraq, the President was very slow to react. Why? Well, my view is that he believed it would all *work out.* Again, that's the mind-set of rich guys. Everything will turn out okay because it has *always* turned out okay.

And the President was not alone in his lack of urgency. On a daily basis, Vice President Cheney, Secretary of Defense Donald Rumsfeld, and others were telling Bush that the problems in Iraq were under control. Why did he believe them? Well, because those men had been correct about the outcome of the Afghan campaign while some other presidential advisers had counseled against a quick anti-Taliban action.

In Iraq, of course, Cheney and Rumsfeld turned out to be wrong.

But beyond policy mistakes, the President did not seem to feel the urgency of the situation, and thus Iraq could very well wind up destroying his legacy. You can also make a case that the same Bush mind-set worsened the Hurricane Katrina situation.

This is cold, not partisan, analysis. Americans are rightly confused and saddened by the Iraq situation. It has cost this country enormous blood and treasure. However, it is important to understand what really happened there. America did nothing immoral by removing a murderous dictator who had violated the first Gulf War cease-fire seventeen times, and who was hell-bent on causing trouble for America. No, the USA did not fail morally; we just weren't very smart in anticipating the complexity of the Iraqi battlefield.

A more apprehensive president—Abraham Lincoln, for example—might have sensed the extent of the debacle sooner than President Bush and acted more swiftly to correct the situation. This is Monday-morning quarterbacking, I know, but if you study Lincoln, you will see a man who reacted to bad news quickly.

I mention President Lincoln because in an extensive private conversation I had with President Bush about Iraq and other matters, Lincoln was on his mind. After I interviewed the former President in October 2006, he invited me to have lunch. I was stunned. Very few people have ever treated me to lunch. It takes great courage.

In the dining room adjacent to the Oval Office, we talked off the record for about thirty minutes. I was impressed by the President's knowledge and analysis of history. He clearly believed that his tough strategy against Islamic extremism had prevented further attacks on U.S. soil and that history would vindicate the Iraq campaign.

You can decide about the President's belief. But I can tell you that personally, he seems to be a good guy. People I trust have told me that he's kind to his staff, generally respectful of the immediate needs of others around him, and much more forgiving of insults than I am.

In fact, I asked the President on camera if he harbored any resentment toward those who hate and spread lies about him. He said no. Then, after the cameras were off, I said something like, "Come on, Mr. President, these people must make you angry."

He just smiled. "They really don't," he replied.

Interviewing a president, as I've said before, is the toughest thing in journalism. There is a line you simply cannot cross because you must respect the office. With everybody else, I can aggressively challenge dubious answers and, within boundaries, even mock them. You may have seen a bit of that in my famous interview with Senator Hillary Clinton. I gave her some jazz that I could never have thrown at the commander in chief. I was respectful but forceful while speaking to Mrs. Clinton.

Talking with a president is obviously a different deal. Certainly, I can challenge, but I can't denigrate the man (or woman) in any way.

If you deviate from being respectful, most of the folks watching will hold it against you no matter what their political bent. That's just the way it is with the commander in chief.

Having a president show you around the White House is somewhat intoxicating, and, of course, the president realizes this. Each room is meticulously cared for, and stories about past presidents abound. If you're like me and study history, there is no more interesting place in the world, with the possible exception of Vatican City. I've visited the White House a number of times and it is always thrilling.

My presidential interviews with Mr. Bush have been major highlights in my long career. In each case, I felt I was fair but tough. In fact, President Bush the elder told me he enjoyed watching the jousts with his son on TV, even though I pushed the President hard to define "coerced interrogation" methods and openly doubted his immigration policy. When Mr. Bush failed to explain exactly how he would secure the southern border, I said directly, "You know, Mr. President, many Americans will not like your answer."

To which he responded, "Well, that's my answer."

Okay.

As for President George Herbert Walker Bush, I have corresponded with him over the years and can tell you the man understands more about how this world works than anyone else I know. Some left-wing writers have speculated that there is tension between the Bushes, that the father and son disagree on some important issues. I have not seen that. I promised to keep President Bush the elder's comments to me private until he dies, and I will keep that promise. He has been kind enough to brief me when I need to know something important about policy, and I greatly appreciate that. As you probably understand, in a world full of deceit and spin, it is very tough to get to the truth of some matters. Having access to a patriot like President George H. W. Bush has, for me, made forming opinions on some vital issues much easier.

By the way, in the lunch I had with the President, I have absolutely no idea what I ate. I simply can't remember. I was so engrossed in the conversation, I could have eaten a caterpillar, for all I know.

President Bill Clinton

Unfortunately, President Clinton has not deemed it necessary to enter the no-spin zone, although I've tried hard to convince him to do so. I've met him and we chatted briefly, but our contact has been mainly between surrogates, and I've never formally interviewed him.

That's a shame, because the conversation would be interesting, and I would value his opinion on a number of issues. In my view, Mr. Clinton sees the world in a unique way but has rarely been challenged in the media, so we don't really know *why* he thinks what he thinks. He's good at making statements, but how he's arrived at his belief system remains a mystery, at least to me. Maybe after he reads this book he'll see the wisdom of speaking to me, just as his wife finally did. Somehow, I don't think Mr. Clinton was ever a bold, fresh guy and may not be fond of my approach. His bestselling autobiography is interesting but doesn't get to the heart of the matter. I'd like to know what's behind the curtain.

President Clinton, of course, is the polar opposite of President George W. Bush. Raised in a working-class broken home, Clinton is as far away from the rich-guy syndrome as you can possibly get. The fact that he rose up from the tiny town of Hope, Arkansas, to become president is astounding. Even those who don't like him have to admit that.

It would be unfair of me to attempt to define how President Clinton wields his power, because I simply don't know. Stories about his temper and sense of entitlement are legion. Stories about my temper are legion. Who the hell knows what's true in his case? So I'm not going to waste your time speculating.

I will say that, from my vantage point, Bill and Hillary Clinton greatly enjoy power. While I never got the feeling that George and Laura Bush woke up every day relishing the perks of their position, I believe the Clintons eat that relish up. I could be wrong.

Covering Bill Clinton's presidency on the *Factor* was a nightmare. After the Lewinsky episode, there was no reasoning with anyone on either side: partisans ran wild; accusations flew like migrating bats. But after a while all the stupid jokes and rank hatred got tedious. Ken Starr was boring. "It's just about sex" was *incredibly* boring. The whole sordid mess seriously damaged the country, but few actually realized what was really going on. While we Americans were wallowing in voyeurism, al Qaeda was killing people overseas and planning greater massacres. Most of us, even in the corridors of power, barely noticed.

Clinton associates have told me that the President often watches the *Factor.* If it's true, I'm glad, and I tell those people to inform the President that he is far more powerful and knowledgeable than I am. Therefore, he should demonstrate that by coming on my program and setting me straight on a number of important issues. If his wife can do it, he can.

President Gerald Ford

Believe me, I tried hard to get President Ford to talk about the impeachment of President Clinton. In phone calls and letters, I tried in every way to get the man on the record about the action. He simply would not offer an opinion.

In a series of interviews conducted for *Parade* magazine (the most widely read weekly publication in the world), I asked President Ford scores of questions about life, liberty, and the pursuit of happiness. At that time, in the fall of 1997, the Clinton scandal was red-hot. Ford was candid on everything but Clinton, telling me that the rules of the "fraternity of former presidents" forbade him to criticize the current chief executive. Since then, both Bill Clinton and especially Jimmy Carter have hammered President Bush hard, so I guess the frat rules have changed for some people.

Anyway, in our chats, I found President Ford to be a nice guy. He did, however, get a bit angry over the fact that his administration has not been praised more. He pointed to the 1975 Helsinki Accords, which stopped Soviet military intrusions in Eastern Europe. Also, he was proud of his work in undermining the South African apartheid system.

The only time President Ford actually got huffy was when I asked about the Richard Nixon pardon. Clearly, he felt he lost the 1976 election to Jimmy Carter because he let Nixon skate on the Watergate mess. But Ford was adamant that he had made the correct decision, saying he had to stop the hatred because it was damaging America. I believe he was right.

I enjoyed talking with President Ford, who, I think, was stimulated by the conversations as well. No question in my mind that he enjoyed his power and status, first as House Speaker, then as president, finally as elder statesman. If we look back on his career, the man tried to do right by his country. He was no visionary or crusader, but he was a patriot.

Gerald Ford, like many presidents, came from a modest background, but once he left the Oval Office, he did not hesitate to amass a fortune by serving on corporate boards and earning enormous speaking fees. As his 2007 tax returns prove, Bill Clinton has done exactly the same thing. Is there anything wrong with that? You make the call.

President Jimmy Carter

It is safe to say that Jimmy Carter has used some of his power to avoid talking to me. About anything. He'll talk with Hamas killers, thereby legitimizing them in the eyes of some folks, but forget about conversing with the bold, fresh guy. I do take this personally.

Over the years, we've invited Mr. Carter on the *Factor* dozens of times, but his "people" barely returned our calls. When they did deign to, I believe there was some sneering going on. This despite the fact that President Carter seems to write a book every three weeks and will appear on cooking shows to promote his work. So there is no question in my mind that Carter does not "get" the bold, fresh guy (whose program sells tons of books for smart authors). Or maybe he does understand and simply despises me. That has been known to happen.

To be fair, President Carter is smart to avoid me, because I think he was a disaster as president. I think he's an okay guy, building those houses for Habitat for Humanity and such, but as the leader of America, the guy was scary.

It all crystallized for me at the 2004 Democratic Convention in Boston. There were President Carter and his wife, Rosalynn, sitting next to Michael Moore, the notorious America basher. The Carters were beaming as TV cameras caught them yukking it up with the rotund provocateur. I mean, think about it: there sat the powerful Jimmy Carter giving his ex-presidential seal of approval to Moore, a man who thinks Fidel Castro is the greatest.

Okay.

There is little more for me to say about Carter. During the hostage crisis, Iran made him look like Little Bo Peep, and on his watch, Americans had to line up for hours to get gas for their cars. Richard Nixon might have been a liar and a crook, but at least he had a clue about the real world and how it works. Carter was given power by the American people and rewarded their judgment by finishing his term looking like Swee'Pea from the Popeye comics. Some guys just can't handle life in the power lane. That was Carter.

Oprah

Okay, it's not even close: Oprah Winfrey is the most powerful woman in the world. Sorry, Hillary. Born into deep poverty in 1954, this woman makes Bill Clinton look like Prince Charles in the humble-beginnings department. Compared to her upbringing in Mississippi, I was raised in the Taj Mahal. And even worse, Ms. Winfrey recalls being molested as a child by several male relatives and friends of her family.

Add it all up and Oprah's climb to the top of the power mountain is simply stunning. No other word for it. So what does this say about America, Michael Moore?

What kind of power does Oprah wield? Well, *Parade* magazine reports that she makes $260 million a year. That's about one million bucks for every day she actually works. Wow.

Basically, earning that kind of money means that Oprah Winfrey can do or buy anything she wants on this earth as long as it's legal and for sale. Like Lola in *Damn Yankees!,* whatever Oprah wants, Oprah gets. Think about that. There are no material limits for Oprah, nothing she cannot afford. Are you still thinking? Does Oprah's situation sound good? Okay, here's the downside: having that kind of money can literally drive a person crazy.

Here's why . . . Remember those glittering Christmas mornings when you were a kid? Mine were thrilling, the highlights of my childhood. The anticipation of getting fun stuff makes most kids happy for weeks. That's why Christmas is magic. Most children experience true joy during that season.

But it was the anticipation, the rarity of the experience that conjured up the magic. If, like Oprah, you can have Christmas every day of the year, there isn't much anticipation, is there? I mean, the thrill of obtaining something exceptional, or unexpected, or long awaited, just doesn't exist. With everything almost instantly available, everything becomes rather ordinary. For that reason, the ultrawealthy, if they are not ultracareful, can become bored, jaded, or, even worse, sadistic or self-destructive. The awful behavior of some celebrities and power brokers illustrates that point beyond a reasonable doubt. Just ask Caligula.

To me, the most interesting part of life is achieving goals and overcoming challenges. If all goals are met and there are no challenges, life can become tedious. That's what Alexander the Great (the bored?) meant by whining, in his early thirties, that there were no more worlds to conquer. The opportunity to experience the most unexpected and best challenges is what gets most human beings up in the morning.

Also, with most of the world struggling in some way, it is not unusual for the very rich to feel very guilty about their material prosperity. "Why do *I* deserve all that comfort?" Along with tedium, that kind of subliminal guilt can consume a person and cause great unhappiness, which is why we see so many self-inflicted wounds among rich folks. Elvis, Ernest Hemingway, Marilyn Monroe, Kurt Cobain, people like that had a lot going for them. Yet, somehow, they chose to destroy themselves. All the fame and money weren't enough.

But back to Oprah. We know each other slightly. For a while, we both worked for King World, a television syndication company, and our paths occasionally crossed. Years later, while promoting *Culture Warrior,* I did a "town meeting" on her Chicago-based talk show. I enjoyed it. Oprah challenged me but also listened to what I had to say. Unlike most in show business, Oprah has been very fair to me.

Because I know people who have worked with her, I have a pretty good idea how Oprah wields her enormous power. From the jump, she's been smart. Anticipating that some people would try to extort money from her, a very common occurrence in the world of the wealthy, she requires employees to sign a "nondisparagement" and confidentiality agreement. Bad-mouth Oprah, you're in court.

In addition, her lawyers are superaggressive in protecting her brand. Use clips of her show without permission, you're in court. I admire how Oprah has used her power to protect herself and her operations. She's shrewd and tough. That's a compliment.

But even Oprah can't derail the tabloid train, so she simply ignores it. Another smart move. Very rarely will you see Ms. Winfrey comment on anything or even consent to be interviewed. Like most truly powerful people, she controls her environment. Good for her.

Most important, she uses her power to help children, and this is where she sets herself apart from most other moguls. In addition to giving millions to help poor and abused kids, Oprah uses her program to encourage society to aggressively protect endangered children. As I write, it is reported that her Angel Network has raised more than $51 million for such causes as Hurricane Katrina relief and educating poor girls in South Africa. Obviously, this is how power *should* be used—to aid those who are most vulnerable to harm and least able to help themselves.

Oprah's program is seen in more than a hundred and thirty countries and continues to dominate American daytime TV. So, if Oprah likes a book, it becomes a best seller. If Oprah likes a recipe, that's what you might be having for dinner. It's a small world, after all, and Oprah is calling some serious shots all around the globe.

Yet in order to remain the most powerful woman in the world, Ms. Winfrey has to be careful. Her endorsement of Senator Barack Obama greatly helped him, no question. But it may not have helped her. Millions of Hillary Clinton supporters as well as many Republicans were not so thrilled when Oprah decided to become a political force. After she rallied for Obama, some polls actually showed Ms. Winfrey losing popularity among the folks. Americans are funny like that; they often admire the successful, but they don't want anyone becoming *too* powerful. That might be the message for Oprah as far as the political arena is concerned.

Nevertheless, I continue to admire what Oprah has chosen to do with her power. When in 2007 a scandal broke out about alleged sexual abuse at the Oprah Winfrey Leadership Academy for Girls, the $40-million school she built near Johannesburg in South Africa, I defended her. While some in the press used the opportunity to cheap-shot Ms. Winfrey, my analysis simply stated that the woman couldn't possibly control the actions of every employee she hires. Those of us who do have power well understand the old adage "No good deed goes unpunished." In South Africa, Oprah tried to do a good thing. Give her a break.

Finally, there is a larger point at play with Oprah. The fact that a black woman from a poor background can command so much power once again illustrates the greatness of America. This could not happen in most other countries. I'm not sure that is widely understood. Regular Americans bestow awesome power on Oprah by watching her TV program and respecting her opinions on a variety of subjects. The folks do this, not the government or some pinhead media executive. And when the people deem you worthy of power, you have been granted both a supreme compliment and a huge responsibility. So far, Oprah has risen to her incredible occasion. She can move the dial on many issues and has often made lives better.

Donald Trump

As far as wielding power goes, the polar opposite of Oprah is Donald Trump, the brash real estate mogul who dabbles in television for his own amusement. But don't underestimate this guy. Trump has the ability to revitalize entire urban neighborhoods, and his operations provide work for hundreds of thousands of Americans. The ability to employ people on a mass scale is a definite power indicator.

Simply put, there is little nuance in Trump's power base; it is derived from cold, hard cash. If money talks, Mr. Trump's lips are exhausted. He controls a huge real estate empire by using a combination of savvy business connections and sheer intimidation.

I've known Trump for years, and he's a true force of nature. Unlike presidents or even Oprah Winfrey, Donald doesn't depend on masses of people for his success or power. No, his enormous clout comes from partnering up with a few high rollers who like his maverick style. They want to invest or live in his buildings, gamble in his casinos, and present a powerful image like Trump does.

Truthfully, I know nothing of Trump's business dealings. That's not my area. Unless he breaks the law, his private dealings are his own business. I've heard he is a ruthless guy. I've heard I'm a ruthless guy. The truth is elusive in these matters—except for me: I can assure you that the bold, fresh guy is the picture of benevolence. However, I may not be objective in this analysis.

Also, I have no idea how Trump wields his power day to day. He looks like a tough guy to me. I mean, it's hard to imagine a man like Trump taking much jazz from anyone. Clearly, he goes out of his way to project an aura of success and confidence. And what you see on TV is what you get in person.

I know this because I have spent some time with Trump. We are both baseball fans, so a couple of times a year, we'll go out to Yankee Stadium and, while watching the game, kick world events around. Trump is well informed and insightful. For example, he understands exactly what I've done with the *Factor* brand because it is similar to what he's done with the Trump brand. In addition to having an acute interest in the world, both Trump and I are well known and exceedingly controversial. So we have common ground.

By the way, I generally keep my social conversations private. If somebody says something to me at a ball game or a dinner, I don't spread it around. Why would I? Gossip is stupid and counterproductive; what my friends tell me stays in Vegas, or in Levittown, or wherever.

But I don't think Donald Trump will mind my analyzing his power, because he himself has done it a number of times in his books. The big thing about Trump is that he gets things done. This is the hallmark of the powerful. When the city of New York dithered around for five years, unable to reconstruct an ice-skating rink in Central Park, Trump stepped in and rehabilitated the Wollman facility in six months. Somehow, he convinced the tough city unions to cooperate and work fast. Very few politicians have ever done that. Check out Boston's "Big Dig" if you don't believe me.

It's the same all over the country. Trump's buildings go up quickly and efficiently, while many public works projects seem to take forever. Why is Trump so much more effective? That's easy: he demands results, and people fear not delivering for him.

So on the surface, at least, you can compare Trump's power to Oprah's in this way: his is driven by trepidation, while her clout is derived from love. But look a bit deeper and you'll see that Oprah is also feared, even though she does not openly work that angle. Nonetheless, it would not be wise for someone in politics or show business to alienate Ms. Winfrey.

Of course, alienating Donald Trump is foolish as well and would very likely lead to a public bloodletting. And it is on this point that I chide him.

Remember that dopey public brawl between Trump and Rosie O'Donnell? It all began in December 2006, after Trump publicly scolded one of his beauty contestants, Miss USA, Tara Connor, for misbehaving. You may have seen the sensational photos that featured Ms. Connor in a variety of salacious poses. There were also allegations of substance abuse.

After the woman agreed to counseling, Trump allowed her to stay in the pageant. However, the situation angered Rosie O'Donnell, who was then cohosting the daytime yak fest *The View* on ABC. Ms. O'Donnell quickly got up close and personal, citing Trump's past tabloid exploits and accusing him of hypocrisy and extreme hubris (which are never good).

Trump immediately fired back, calling Ms. O'Donnell an astonishing variety of names, including a "big, fat pig" and "a mental midget."

Rosie, rising to the challenge as only she can, rejoined that Trump was a "pimp" and a "degenerate."

While even the Little Rascals would have been embarrassed, the jaded media swooned with joy.

Then Mr. Trump announced he was going to sue Ms. O'Donnell. That's when I booked him on the *Factor*. The following is a partial transcript of the conversation, where I try to convince Trump that getting down in the mud with O'Donnell is not helping him.

O'Reilly: Don't you understand that Rosie is making herself look bad?

Trump: Hey, Bill, there are two types of people in this world—people that take it and people that don't take it. Rosie is a bully.

O'Reilly: All right, so I'm not going to be able to convince you to beat her intellectually and to stay out of the personal.

Trump: This is ultimately intellectual. You know, I went to the best school. I went to the Wharton School of Finance.

O'Reilly: That's what I'm telling you. Why do you have to talk about her girlfriend then? Just talk about the erroneous things she says.

Trump: I feel sorry for her. I'm not talking about her girlfriend. I feel sorry for her girlfriend. How would you like to have to kiss Rosie?

O'Reilly: That's what I'm talking about. You don't need to do that.

Trump: I feel sorry for this girl. I just found out her name is Kelly. She looks like a lovely young woman. Too bad she got stuck with Rosie.

O'Reilly: Okay. Now, the lawsuit. You can't win, and I'll tell you why. You have to prove damages, and you're not going to be able to prove damages.

Trump: You know, Bill, do me a favor. Don't be my lawyer.

O'Reilly: Have you thought about that?

Trump: I think about everything.

O'Reilly: You can show malice, but not prove damages.

Trump: Bill, don't be my lawyer. I like you. You're my friend. Don't be my lawyer.

O'Reilly: Can I be your adviser?

Trump: Yes.

O'Reilly: Don't use any more personal attacks.

Trump: I will take that very seriously.

Okay.

A few days after that interview, the spat died and, ultimately, Trump did not sue. However, I think it is safe to say that the entire sordid joust energized and satisfied him.

You see, Donald Trump believes that even cheap publicity enhances his power and brand because it gets his name "out there." But he is wrong. Rosie O'Donnell has no power whatsoever. She can huff and puff all day long, but nothing much will change. As with most entertainers, Rosie works because others more powerful than she is allow her to work. She and ninety-nine percent of other show business people are hired mercenaries whose plug can be pulled at any time.

So, by publicly slugging it out with Rosie, Trump elevated her to his power level, while at the same time sinking into "the no-class zone." Does that sound smart to you? Remember, Trump controls his operations; he doesn't need the approval of some TV mogul to get paid. He is a thousand times more powerful than Rosie O'Donnell will ever be. Very simply, he should have issued a statement that Ms. O'Donnell was misguided and misinformed about the pageant controversy, and said nothing else.

In fact, you have to think long and hard to find any entertainer with real power. The lead singer of U2, Bono, does have the ability to raise big money for charity and right some societal wrongs, but he is a rarity. Most celebrities are, basically, just temporary diversions for the folks. Usually, the famous don't understand that, but truly powerful people should. For some reason, Donald Trump engages in feuds with folks far below him on the power scale. He should re-think that. As we all know, fame is fleeting, and so is power. When you have it, you should use it to do some good. Call me crazy, but I don't think trading insults with Rosie O'Donnell falls into that category.

Also, there are some concerns that might do business with Donald Trump but are afraid to do so because, if anything goes south, they might be on the receiving end of some Rosie-type treatment. Trump should consider that.

I do agree with Trump that there are two kinds of people in the world, and if you are being mistreated, you *should* fight back. But there are a variety of ways in which to wage combat. As I've stated, before the *Factor* publicly goes after somebody, we try to reason with them behind the scenes. It is only when they reject the soft approach that we go in hard.

In the O'Donnell case, I did have to take the woman on a few times myself, because she is basically out of control. But we did it strictly on issues. As mentioned, when she implied that the 9/11 attack was an inside job, we used a study by Purdue University that analyzed the World Trade Center damage to illustrate just how crazy Rosie's words really were. We did not call her fat.

Finally, there is nothing wrong with Trump or any powerful person calling attention to unfairness or just plain nonsense. I do it all the time, and wish more powerful people would step up. When a powerful person publicly points to wrongdoing, that wrongdoing gets some exposure in the media. Obviously, that is a good thing. Too many powerful Americans use their status simply to help themselves. That is a bad thing.

Bill O'Reilly

Once in a while a friend will ask me something like, "O'Reilly, do you know how powerful you are?" That kind of question brushes the bold, fresh guy back a bit. I just never think about my job in that way. Of course, I can affect some lives, and as I mentioned, I'm always careful about my actions in that regard. But the fact that I hold some power does not really mean much to me.

Besides, when it comes to what other people are doing with their lives, I've always been a libertarian kind of guy. As long as you're not hurting anyone, have a good time. Sure, I have my philosophy and gravitate toward people who see life the way I do, but I am not a missionary. I'll put forth my case on a belief or issue, stand back, and let you decide its merits. Even though I'd like you to see it my way, I am not in the persuasion business. And I don't dislike people who see life differently than I do, as long as they are sincere.

The power deal, however, does have its moments. Because I'm seen and heard by millions every day, opportunities to do some good come along quite often. Here's just one small example. In March 2007, the *Factor* learned that a ten-year-old Iowa girl was dying of a brain tumor. Her only wish was to see her incarcerated father one last time. Unfortunately, the man was serving federal time in North Dakota, about five hundred miles from his daughter. A convicted drug dealer, he had asked for a special furlough, but the warden had turned him down.

My investigators looked at the situation and it quickly crystallized. The father had just about completed his sentence, and freedom was just a few months away. Also, a federal judge had no problem with the supervised visit, and furloughs of this kind had been granted in the past. So I went on the air and politely, but firmly, asked the warden to reconsider.

He did. The girl and the father had their visit. She died a few days later.

Shortly after that, an old friend of mine called to say that the story had made her cry. She thanked me for doing it and said she believes this is why I have been granted the good fortune of national success. I agree. That's why I try to use my power in this direction as much as I can. We are tough on the *Factor,* but we're also compassionate and believe in redemption. Our record over the years proves it.

As for the perks of power, they are fine, I guess. I don't really care much about them, even though it's nice to get good seats at events and be able to travel quickly without hassle. But, basically, it's the work that I enjoy, not the benefits that come from the work. Whenever I see a famous person acting like a jerk, I cringe. I hope I never insult the folks by acting like I'm above them in some way. If I do, let me know immediately.

Summing up this chapter, it is clear to me that many people crave power and influence, but few really have it. Those who do acquire power either derive it from the folks or grab it by getting their hands on big money. Either way, all of the really powerful people have an obligation to make the world a better place, and those who don't are subject to scrutiny from the *Factor.* That's how I use my power.

By the way, my seventh-grade teacher, Sister Thomas, did go out of her way to emphasize that it is harder for a rich man to enter the kingdom of heaven than it is for a camel to pass through the eye of a needle. (Possibly a reference to a small needle's-eye door in the

Jaffa Gate of the Jerusalem wall, although some Christians take the Bible passage literally.) I recall Clement's reaction to that lesson was to say he was glad you could get cigarettes (Camel brand) in heaven or some stupid thing. But you get the idea: wealth and fame and clout look great from a distance, but, again, be careful what you wish for.

Power to the people, indeed. But understand it's a very hot plate.

14

MYSTERIES OF THE UNIVERSE

Don't try to plan me
Or understand me,
I can't stand to be understood.

—THE TURTLES, "LET ME BE"

Y ou might want to skip this chapter. Or maybe read it very fast. No
question, it's the most ridiculous part of the entire book. No spin.

You see, I am a popular culture vulture and have been ever since
Davy Crockett and Georgie Russell were roaming around on the
Disney show back in the 1950s. And over the years, there have been
a number of pop-culture things that, for a variety of reasons, I simply do not understand. With some remorse, I have chosen to drop
some of these mysteries on you. I'm sorry. I shouldn't be doing this.
But I can't help it. It's just who the bold, fresh guy is.

The singer Paul Simon, who's a few years older than your humble correspondent, has stated that he believes he was born at exactly
the right time; that, over the years, he has experienced great change
in nearly every decade of his life. Simon, in my estimation, is right
on. From the advent of rock 'n' roll; to the turbulent antiwar sixties,

including the sexual revolution; to the disco seventies; to the high-tech world we have right now, it seems like the baby boomers have surfed the crest of every wave that washed in dramatic change.

That's why I'm glad I'm a boomer, grateful to have experienced so much. But, along the way, certain things have struck me as inexplicable. These events, people, and beliefs have stayed with me because they are totally beyond my comprehension. As you are about to find out, most of them are trivial and demonstrate the level of immaturity that I must live with every day. Pray for me.

The following ramblings are not in any particular order; I'm just going along with my personal stream of consciousness. Again, I apologize.

Let's begin with Brad Pitt, a complete mystery of the universe to me. I am definitely not understanding "Pittmania" and the attention this man gets. Good-looking guy, sure, and he's a pretty good actor (but if you can miss the movie *Troy,* by all means do so). However, Brad Pitt commands millions in salary and is in the entertainment press almost daily. Why? Yes, he's involved with Angelina Jolie, and that union became notorious because Pitt divorced actress Jennifer Aniston (who seems like a nice woman) to make it happen. But so what? All of that occurred years ago, and despite a mediocre movie résumé, Mr. Pitt is still a huge star. Again, not getting this at all.

On the music front, Madonna bugs me. Her early songs are catchy, and I like the fact that she came from humble Michigan roots before rising to the top of the charts. According to *Forbes* magazine, she's now worth about $350 million; quite an achievement for a working-class girl. But, somehow along the way, Madonna has succumbed to the awful disease of pretension. The latest symptom is her phony English accent. What is that all about? Is there no one alive who can tell Madonna that, when she talks these days, she sounds like a transsexual version of Peter Sellers? Annoying? Off the chart.

Next up is television. As a kid, I did not get Captain Kangaroo. When this guy came on, I left the room. I understand the actor who played him, Bob Keeshan, was a good guy in real life and that millions of kids loved the Captain. But all I saw was a boring old guy who roamed around doing little of consequence. The bad haircut and cheap sweater didn't help either. I much preferred the double-entendre king Soupy Sales, which should tell you a lot about the bold, fresh guy.

Still with me? There's plenty more. In the late summer of 1965 everybody was singing the number one hit song, "Hang on Sloopy," by the McCoys. Everybody, that is, except me. I simply could not get past the incredibly dumb central theme. Sloopy sounded like a dog's name. To this day, I have never heard of a human being named Sloopy.

Truly, the words of this song drove me nuts.

Sloopy, I don't care what your daddy do.
'Cause you know, Sloopy, girl, I'm in love with yoooouuuu.

"I don't care what your daddy do"? Are you kidding me? Good grief. The song stayed in the top forty for eleven weeks, and during that time I broached with my parents the subject of possibly moving to Argentina.

Almost as bad was my guy Elvis singing a song called "Do the Clam." That incredible travesty also happened in 1965, and it hurt me deeply. By that time, I had accepted the fact that the big E was

living in a daze, starring in films like *Harum Scarum* and *Kissin'
Cousins.* But *Girl Happy* was the absolute worst. In that movie, Elvis sang the following lyrics. They made my head hurt:

> Do the clam, do the clam,
> Grab your barefoot baby by the hand.

And not only did Elvis warble those words; he did so while wearing a white suit and black shoes. My God.

On the political scene, Vice President Spiro Agnew was a complete
mystery of the universe. His friends called him Ted, and for some
unknown reason, Richard Nixon selected "Ted" to be his running
mate in 1968. And they actually won the White House twice! But,
again, be careful what you wish for. In 1973, Ted was indicted for
federal income tax evasion and was forced to resign, barely slither-
ing out of a prison sentence. It turned out that Ted had raked in a
total of $268,482 in bribes from builders while he was governor of
Maryland. Nice. And when he asked the bribe givers to keep paying him in the veep's office, they got teed off and called the feds.
Eventually, investigators proved him to be a hard-core crook, as was
Nixon. But at least Nixon knew stuff. Ted just ran around calling
the press "nattering nabobs of negativism." Which is true, but, hey,
you've got to bring more to the table than *that.*

When I asked my father about Agnew, he said just one word:
"Clown."

As I mentioned, I saw many monster movies as a kid. And like Bill
Murray's gang, the Ghostbusters, who were ready to believe anyone

who would pay them to find spirits, I was always ready to believe what was up there on the screen. Dracula, for sure, was not a guy to be messed with, but there were lots of crosses in my house, so he wasn't much of a threat to me. The Invisible Man did not haunt me; I'm not exactly sure why. And Frankenstein's monster was over there in Bavaria someplace and not likely to book a transatlantic flight anytime soon.

It was the Mummy, though, that drove me crazy. In the original 1932 film, Boris Karloff came back to life after some English guys violated the tomb of an ancient Egyptian princess. Okay, fine, I'm buying the curse business that forced Karloff to rise from his sarcophagus. But here's the problem: the Mummy was slow . . . very . . . very . . . slow. It took him three days to do the hundred-yard dash. And, unlike Dracula, he couldn't hypnotize you with his eyes, because they were covered with dusty bandages. Are you getting the picture? So anybody could simply run away from the Mummy—he couldn't catch Mount Rushmore. But every time Boris showed up, his victim just stood there screaming. Didn't try to run at all. The person *just let the Mummy walk up and strangle him.* This was insane.

I remember loudly saying to my friends during the movie, "Why doesn't the guy just run away?" Other moviegoers shushed me, but it was a legitimate question. All of us should have demanded refunds.

Tiny Tim also drove me nuts. Not the Dickens character in *The Christmas Carol,* but a guy from Brooklyn named Herbert Khaury who showed up on the Johnny Carson program singing a song called "Tiptoe Through the Tulips." Khaury used the name Tiny Tim, and was as revolting a presence as I've ever seen on TV. Strumming a stupid ukulele and showing off long, stringy, unkempt hair, the Tiny guy was a train wreck. But Carson loved him and made him a star, at least for the year 1968. As you may remember, Tiny "married" a woman called Miss Vicki on Carson's show, capping off as bizarre a career as has ever been seen in this country. By the way, about 40 million Americans viewed the unbelievably hyped "wedding." More, even, than watch the *Factor.*

Not much better was *The Beverly Hillbillies.* Again, inexplicable. This program, along with *Green Acres* and *Gilligan's Island,* insulted the word *dumb,* but, for some reason, millions of Americans could not stop watching. I cannot explain this, and it has disturbed me since childhood.

See, most of the time, I really do understand why things happen in our culture. In matters of entertainment, individual tastes obviously rule. For example, I like the Bee Gees, because, to me, their tunes and harmonies are pleasing. But lots of folks hate the Brothers Gibb, believing their songs to be trite. I can relate to that, but obviously, trite doesn't much bother me.

On the other hand, I could never listen to a group like Metallica. Not for a minute. But millions of folks like the heavy-metal stuff, and I have no problem with that. Every person hears sound in a unique way. But, let's face it, there is no excuse for a group called the 1910 Fruitgum Company, whose first single, "Simon Says," rose to number two in 1968. A cultural tragedy if there ever was one.

In 1970, I walked out of a movie called *Love Story.* It was just too much. Ali MacGraw and Ryan O'Neal, madly infatuated, mouthing lines like, "Love means never having to say you're sorry." Awful, and what does that mean, exactly? I step on your foot and don't apologize because I'm in love? "Oh, I stepped on your toes, madam;

forgive me because I can't apologize. I made out with Ali MacGraw last night and can never apologize for anything ever again."

Back then, the ladies at Vassar College were buying this *Love Story* stuff big-time, but the thugs living with me at Marist College were having none of it. In fact, any guy who liked that film was immediately mocked and scorned beyond belief. To Marist's everlasting honor, approving of *Love Story* was a campus career breaker.

Later, I learned that Al Gore, a student at Harvard when *Love Story* author Erich Segal taught there, may have been the inspiration for the lead character. And even though Al was rumored to have embraced the *Love Story* speculation, it is brutally unfair to him because, I believe, all the hot air spewed in that movie was the beginning of the global warming crisis. And I resent that very much.

Perhaps the worst movie I've ever seen was *Moment to Moment,* a 1978 bomb starring John Travolta and Lily Tomlin. *Moment to Moment* makes *Love Story* look like *Citizen Kane.*

For mental health reasons, I've tried to block this movie out of my mind, but I do remember Ms. Tomlin, fifteen years Travolta's senior, getting into a hot tub with him. Was Ruth Buzzi not available? Anyway, Travolta was wearing a Speedo, and Lily was, well, appreciating him. All I can say is that this was not a high point in the history of heterosexuality. Also, I kept wondering what the *Welcome Back, Kotter* guys, the Sweathogs, would say.

A few years later, Travolta starred in another hydrogen bomb called *Perfect.* In this one, he and Jamie Lee Curtis work out in a health club and fall in love amid the free weights. I kept waiting for someone to say, "Love means never having to do aerobics." But it never happened. In fact, nothing really happened. Unless you count Jamie Lee perspiring in skintight gym clothes, which, believe me, is no small thing.

After the *Perfect* embarrassment, Travolta did not make another film for four years. Then, in 1989, he made a comeback with a baby movie called *Look Who's Talking.* Good for him. Even though he has a definite karma debt for *Moment to Moment* and *Perfect,* I'm glad the guy made it back.

It is truly a mystery of the universe as to how some movies get made. These days, few Americans even bother going to the theater unless they want to keep their little kids quiet with a dose of *Shrek.* Hollywood moguls, understanding that computers provide a vast array of at-home entertainment for Americans, now make most movies for people in Bangladesh. That explains the return of *Rambo.*

Looking back, during the late 1960s and early 1970s there were unexplained expositions nearly every day. For example, in the fall of 1967 a song called "Incense and Peppermints" hit number one. The group that sang the song was called Strawberry Alarm Clock. What does that name mean? Why not call the group Cinnamon Raisin Toast? I mean, people were so fried back then that anything was acceptable as long as it was "far out."

My theory is that folks got so fed up with the 1960s "psychedelic rock" that, in desperation, they turned to disco. Tell me that listening to Vanilla Fudge or Iron Butterfly won't make you crazy after a while. So, with insanity in the wind, *Saturday Night Fever* arrived on the scene.

Actually, that blockbuster 1977 movie, starring the aforementioned John Travolta, was an excellent depiction of working-class Brooklyn in those days. I completely understand the film's success. But the societal craze it spawned requires some deep thought, some of it very painful.

No question but that some disco tunes were catchy and vibrant. And, take it from me, it was fun to go out and make a complete fool of yourself on the dance floor. Thus, at the height of the disco craze in the late 1970s, you had college graduates actually singing along with KC and the Sunshine Band:

That's the way, uh-huh uh-huh,
I like it, uh-huh, uh-huh.
That's the way, uh-huh uh-huh,
I like it, uh-huh, uh-huh.

If you buy the album, you'll hear that chorus at least ninety-seven times in the course of the song. Can you explain that to me?

The disco era crashed and died in the mid-eighties, but not before Donna Summer, the Village People, and KC burned their images into the fabric of America. Go to any wedding reception today and say hello to them for me.

Hands down, the worst hit song I have ever heard, and that includes the Sloopster, is the Willie Nelson–Julio Iglesias atrocity "To All the Girls I've Loved Before." Arrest warrants should have been sworn out immediately after that turkey hit the marketplace.

In the interest of full disclosure, I should tell you that I interviewed Willie Nelson way back in 1977. As a young reporter in Dallas, I was sent out to get his take on something or other. I can't remember exactly what. However, I do recall that during the interview, which took place on his bus, Nelson smoked pot and waved a pistol around. That didn't faze me much, but it was weird, no question.

Anyway, in 1984, Nelson and Iglesias, a rather smarmy Latin ballad singer, put out this song that congratulates women on sleeping with them. The big line in the recording is "We're glad they came along." Now, I'm no feminist or anything, but that sounds just a wee bit condescending. Does it not? "We're glad they came along"? Just for laughs, run that by some ladies and see how they react.

Yet, incredibly, the song hit number one on the country chart and spent three months on the pop chart, peaking at number five. If there's a bigger mystery in the universe, please let me know.

But wait, I might have found a bigger one. In 1980, Willie Nelson appeared in a movie called *Honeysuckle Rose* along with actress Dyan Cannon. At the time, Ms. Cannon was forty-three years old and a great-looking woman. I didn't see the film, but I understand that Dyan, who was once married to Cary Grant, and Nelson actually hooked up romantically! The only thing I can figure out is that the movie studios mixed up *Honeysuckle Rose* and *Moment to Moment*. It was *supposed* to be Dyan Cannon romancing John Travolta and Lily Tomlin with Willie Nelson. Now, that might sound unfair to Ms. Tomlin, but there is no other credible explanation.

Currently, there are many cultural mysteries still in play. For one, I know people who can watch six hours of *American Idol* a week. They call one another and talk about some young girl from Rhode Island who sings "Respect" and then gets heckled by Simon Cowell. Again, if anyone can explain this, please write.

Dancing with the Stars is big, too. Once, a guy named Tucker Carlson appeared on that program and did the mambo or something. Carlson is a political commentator on TV who has not been very successful. I watched Carlson dancing on that program. This tape should be airlifted to Guantánamo Bay for interrogation use.

You may know that a rapper named Snoop Dogg has made millions of dollars. He used to call himself "Snoop Doggy Dogg," but dropped the Doggy. No one knows why. One of his big hits includes the phrase "I want'a do something freaky to you." Actually, I've never heard this song, but that lyric sounds great, doesn't it? Nat King Cole, I'm sure, would have loved it.

By the way, Mr. Dogg's mom appeared on the *Factor.* Nice woman. She said that her son, whose given name is Calvin Broadus Jr., is nice to her. Beyond that, she can't imagine why he's been arrested so many times but believes it might be a mis-understanding of some kind.

Vice President Dick Cheney is a complete mystery to me. I inter-viewed him back in 1990, and that was it. He would never again consent to be interviewed by the bold, fresh guy. During my one chat with Cheney, I pushed him on why the press didn't like him. In fact, the press despises Cheney so much they'd rather dine with the late Idi Amin. Cheney would not concede the loathing.

The main problem with Cheney and, to a lesser extent, with Presi-dent Bush is that they rarely explain themselves to "we, the people." When Iraq went south, Cheney went hunting. Not very responsible, since he was one of the prime "get Saddam" guys. He should have been out there explaining what the hell was going on. But he didn't. The result? His MIA status allowed NBC News and the *New York Times* to define the issue. Disastrous. Also, not fair to brave men and women fighting in that conflict, and not fair to their families here at home. Cheney should have stood up.

Call me crazy, but I'd like all elected officials to be stand-up guys and gals. If you make a mistake, admit it. If the going gets tough, ex-plain. Cheney essentially hid out for eight years in his lavish Wash-ington residence and now will retire to his lavish Wyoming residence with a handsome pension paid for by you and me. We deserved more for our money.

By the way, I've sat close to Dick Cheney at two Washington dinners. He is a smart and witty man. But he's kept that very secret, hasn't he? Another mystery.

Will someone please explain why ultrafortunate entertainment people abuse the regular folks who have made them rich and famous? This is an amazing phenomenon, and the two best examples of it are *Seinfeld* and *The Sopranos.*

You may remember that in the final episode of *Seinfeld,* the wacky cast wound up in some small-town jail. It was not funny. After nine years of clever writing and brilliant comedic acting, Seinfeld's closing act rivaled *Petticoat Junction* in witty payoff. So what the heck happened?

Since I'm pretty sure I understand the deep cynicism of head writer Larry David and also the middling cynicism of Jerry Seinfeld, I think these guys tanked the final episode on purpose. Perhaps they were simply tired of all the show-closing hype and went out to lunch. The last show was definitely a big "whatever." There is no other explanation, especially if you acknowledge what *could* have happened.

Using Johnny Carson's brilliant last program as a model, all the *Seinfeld* people had to do was assemble the cast for a one-hour "best moments" special. Just let the characters kick it around, telling viewers what mattered to them and why, and then roll in the clips. Give the folks some inside-baseball as to how the show came together each week, and then wrap it up with some bloopers. David and Seinfeld could have outlined that slam-dunk show in ten minutes.

Instead, they produced a dud final episode that the scriptwriters for *My Mother the Car* would have rejected.

The Sopranos was even worse. Here we had a multiweek story arc that viewers closely followed. Millions of people invested their time and were looking forward to some kind of resolution and pay-off in the last episode. If you are a fan of the program, you know that low-level gangster Tony Soprano, played brilliantly by James Gandolfini, was a ruthless but not totally evil criminal, a compli-cated man whom many viewers thought about even after the epi-sodes ended.

So, after seven seasons on the air, expectations of the show's cli-max were running incredibly high. Would the feds get Tony? Would other mobsters take him out? Would his family be harmed? What would finally happen to the big guy?

Nothing, that's what.

The producer of *The Sopranos,* David Chase, totally punted. In the final scene, Tony and his family were eating at some New Jersey diner while an ominous-looking guy glared at them from across the restaurant. Fade to black. Fade to stupid. I was outraged, and I be-lieve I was not alone. I sat there in my living room wanting to take out a contract on Mr. Chase.

But, hey, I was stupid as well. I expected the creative minds be-hind *Seinfeld* and *The Sopranos* to consider the expectations of the audience. After all, as I noted earlier, it is those people who make people like Jerry Seinfeld, Larry David, David Chase, and their cast members rich and famous. How about looking out for the folks and giving them an enjoyable send-off?

Forget it.

Perhaps I'm wrong, but I believe what happened on *Seinfeld* and *The Sopranos* demonstrates a condescending contempt for the au-dience that is common in Hollywood. What other explanation is there? All the producers had to do was test the final episodes for a selected group of viewers (commonly done in the TV industry), and they could have instantly found out they were not delivering the goods.

But I believe they knew that from the jump. Those people are smart. They just didn't care.

Of course, these are only TV programs, and they don't really matter much in the big scheme of things. But what those guys did was not *fair* to the audience. "Fair"—now, that's an interesting concept. "Fair" is the reason I'm even discussing *Seinfeld* and *The Sopranos*. You see, imposing a sense of fairness on the world is what drives me in my profession and, basically, in my life. And the same might even be true for you.

CHAPTER

AND JUSTICE FOR ALL

Life is not fair.

—UNIVERSAL PARENTAL MANTRA

S o, we've come this far, and I appreciate your patience with my ramblings. Because the Pew Research organization and others have stated that my viewers, listeners, and readers are generally well informed and educated, by now you have undoubtedly picked up a central theme in this book: I do not like to see people treated unfairly (including me). And I will use my power to right what I perceive as wrongs. Of course, many people do not see the wrongs that I see because they don't see the world the way that I do. All of us should feel very sorry for them.

At some time, every kid in the world feels his or her parents are being unfair. That usually happens after the parent prevents the kid from putting the cat in the microwave. The kid, of course, means no harm, but at four years old, little Ashley may not completely understand the consequences of her actions.

Like me, I'm sure you occasionally whined to your folks about the unfairness factor. Actually, I didn't do it all that much, because in my house, it was a road to nowhere. My father was *proud* of being unfair. If I felt his regulations were not in my best interest, he wasn't bothered in the least.

In fact, he often wouldn't even have the conversation. When I approached him with some complaint, he'd listen for about twenty seconds and then either leave the room without comment or simply say, "Can't help you."

Okay.

But once in a *rare* while, when I actually had put together a cogent argument, my father would revise family policy. I can't exactly recall an incident when that actually happened, but my mother swears it did.

School was another story. There, fairness was constantly debated, and the nuns, like President Bush, were the "deciders" of justice. This was not good.

Take my big fight with Tommy M. in the sixth grade. I can't remember exactly what sparked the fracas, but it had been brewing. Tommy was a teacher's pet, and I was a miniature John Dillinger. I did not like Tommy's coziness with our teacher, Mrs. Boyle, and he objected to my objection. A bad moon was definitely rising.

When it came, the fight was fierce. Real punches were thrown, shirts were ripped, blood was drawn. This was shocking at St. Brigid's School, since most playground confrontations were foolish exercises in pushing and name-calling.

"You're a clod!"

"I know you are, but what am I?"

With material like that, most combatants quickly drifted into a deflated state, and the conflict harmlessly petered out. But this dustup with Tommy was a far different story. It was nasty.

Mrs. Boyle, an elderly woman whose heavily made-up face resembled that of Phyllis Diller, was appalled and angered upon seeing me and Tommy stumble into the classroom after round ten. She immediately sent us to the principal's office, where we were to be judged by a feared nun named Sister Thomasine (no relation to Sister Thomas), whom I mentioned in chapter five.

But the good sister had a problem: Tommy's father, a doctor, was a big-time donor to the church. Punishing his kid, a straight-A student, would not be easy. I, the bold, fresh guy, could be sent to Devil's Island without much consequence, but Sister Thomasine had to be cautious with Tommy.

After hearing both our "sides," the sister announced the verdict: banishment to the convent (the place the nuns actually lived), where piles of busywork would be heaped upon us. But there was one thing further: Tommy got just one day of convent hell, while I received *two* days. For previous violations, the sister stated.

Outrage gripped me. I had *already* been punished for those "previous" violations. After watching *Perry Mason,* I knew this was double jeopardy or something. But, above all, IT WASN'T FAIR!

Upon hearing the verdict, Clement rose to my defense and, in no uncertain terms, publicly condemned the sentence, throwing in something about Jesus not liking it as well. That outburst got Clem sent to the convent along with Tommy and me. Thinking back, I believe that's what Clement had in mind all along.

Now, you have to picture this: the nuns who taught at St. Brigid's School lived in an old stone convent on Post Avenue in Westbury. The building is still there. To a dopey sixth grader, it looked big and spooky. When I drive by it today, it looks small and quaint.

An ancient nun named Sister Gerardo guarded the convent. She was too old to teach, so she stayed in the stone building all day and, I assume, prayed diligently for bad boys like me. When Tommy, Clem, and I showed up for detention, the old sister just stared and mumbled something about behaving.

Sure.

Sister Gerardo quickly assigned us to our punishment desks, which were sensibly located in separate rooms. There, mountains of math problems and composition stuff lay awaiting our attention. This was bad. Real bad.

The first day passed slowly and painfully. At three in the afternoon we were released, with Tommy smirking at Clem and me. He was finished with his sanction, but we had another day of solitary confinement. No matter, Clem and I agreed that Tommy would get his down the road.

The next day Sister Gerardo repeated the drill. However, about an hour into the imprisonment, I heard a sharp "pssst." There in the convent hallway stood Clem.

"Billy, she's asleep. The nun. She's out."

I got up and peeked into a side room down the hall. It was true. Sister Gerardo sat there motionless, head drooping, mind off someplace in the Land of Nod.

"Let's check this place out," Clem whispered.

Check this place out? This was the convent where the nuns ate and slept. *Nobody* checked that out.

"They'll kill us if we get caught," I said quietly.

Clem just laughed. "Come on."

Creeping along the creepy corridor, Clem and I looked in every room. There was nothing too unusual about the place: a big kitchen, dining room, a couple of parlors, one of which was occupied by the sleepy sister.

Then Clem went insane.

"Let's go upstairs."

"What? Upstairs to where they *sleep*?"

"Yeah, come on."

Now, once again you have to picture this. Above all, Catholic schoolkids were taught strict boundaries. The places where priests and nuns lived were waaaaaaay out of bounds. If what Clem was suggesting wasn't a mortal sin, then nothing was.

"No way," I said.

"Billy, come on; nobody will ever find out. Chicken?"

There it was . . . the C-word. For boys in my circumstance, trial by fire. Chicken. Awful. With grave doubts, I followed Clem up the stairs.

Sweating heavily, I remember walking down the narrow hallway and peering into the tiny rooms on both sides. All the doors were open. Inside each one I saw a small bed, like my sister's, a tall chest of drawers, and a closet. The rooms were pretty much identical. Crucifixes hung over the beds. Jesus was looking directly *at me.*

"Okay, we did it. Let's get out of here," I said to Clem. I believe I was pleading.

To this day, I have not forgotten the demented gleam that appeared in his eyes. He shook his head no and entered one of the rooms. Let me repeat: HE ENTERED ONE OF THE ROOMS WHERE A NUN SLEPT! My God.

Terrified, I split. I simply spun on my heel and walked quickly but quietly down the stairs and back to my jail desk. Sister Gerardo was still out. A few minutes later, Clement looked into my room, wearing a crazed smile. I did not want to know.

A few hours later, Clem and I were released from captivity by Sister Thomasine, who threatened further pain if we continued to be "disruptive."

Walking out of the building, Clem began laughing.

"I saw their underwear."

Shocked, I just stared at him.

"Yeah, it's white. I took some of it out of a drawer and hid it under one of the beds."

For one of the few times in my life, I was speechless. What could any eleven-year-old kid say? Clement had removed a nun's undergarments from her drawer and hid them under a bed. I believe this was the first time in Catholic school history that a sacrilege like that had ever happened.

Slowly, my thought processes, such as they were, returned.

"Look, Clem. Don't tell anybody you did that, okay? We'll get expelled, and that's just the beginning."

My father's face popped into my mind and was quickly replaced by hellfire.

Clem did not answer right away. Terror grew inside me. But then he said the sweetest words in the world: "Okay, Billy, I won't tell anybody."

And he didn't, as far as I know.

But for weeks afterward, every time my mother or father called my name, I jumped. Every time I saw Sister Thomasine, I dived for cover. Paranoia does not even begin to cover this.

The great convent caper never came back to bite me. It was one of the few times in my life that I did something untoward and didn't get hammered for it. I never heard anything about any nun's clothing. Maybe Clement made the whole thing up. But I wouldn't bet on it.

Eventually, I came to realize that some of the unfairness that I experienced at St. Brigid's was actually fair in a roundabout way. Since all the teachers knew that Clem and I were constantly causing trouble, they obviously felt payback on their part was logical and, mostly, proportionate. On balance, we did get away with a lot of petty stuff.

Think about your own life in this regard. I bet you remember some times when you were treated unfairly. Everybody does. But it's how you handle the unfairness in life that may dictate your success or failure. Dealing effectively with inevitable unfair play is not taught in any classroom, as far as I know, and it should be.

Here's my take. It took me years to figure out that there are essentially three ways to handle unfair situations. You can ignore them, as my mother usually did. You can confront them directly, as I often do. Or you can deal with them after the fact, using well-thought-out strategy.

Unfortunately, most people take the first route. Even though it may anger them, they accept an unfair situation as inevitable. They hold things inside them. Of course, that breeds resentment and bitterness. But some folks can absorb a lot of punishment, as we all know. But it's not physically or mentally healthy to do that.

Deciding to confront unfairness head-on usually leads to a "situation," and if you don't have the power to win the fight, you could wind up in the convent, so to speak. That was my signature move. I'd take on martinets who had far more power than I did and I'd lose. Often, I didn't care. I looked at myself as a crusader for justice and that was that. To my credit, I was willing to take the hits, since it was my decision to confront that provoked many of them. If I was treated unfairly at my job, I found another job. If somebody was giving me a hard time, they got the hard time right back.

Do I regret that strategy? Yes and no. Some conflicts have made me stronger, no question. But had I taken a more patient approach to righting a wrong, I could have won a lot more of those confrontations and saved myself considerable pain.

Scores of books, like *The Art of War,* will teach you conflict strategy, but for me the issue of fairness swings both ways. If you want to be treated righteously, then you must be righteous to others. That's true, even when it's a pain in the rear to do that. Nobody is perfect, but I strive to be fair for one very compelling reason: I know how it feels to be treated unfairly.

If you Google my name, you will find millions of items. Some are as vile as anything ever said about anybody. I usually ignore them, except when they originate from institutions that actually have power. Then I deal with the situation. See, I know if those people are unfairly attacking me, they'll do the same thing to others who are more vulnerable. And my job is to hold the powerful accountable for their actions. So I do my job.

Sometimes, however, there is wisdom in fighting unfairness and injustice with patience, biding your time so that all your options become clear. For example, in the spring of 1985, I was anchoring

the news at KATU-TV in Portland, Oregon. The situation was interesting. I had signed a short, one-year contract to replace a longtime
Oregon anchorman who was retiring. Hoping to attract younger
viewers, station management brought in a hotshot from the East
Coast and paid him big money.

That hotshot was the bold, fresh guy.

Predictably, some in the newsroom were not fond of hotshots,
and so a kind of station culture war erupted. The younger folks liked
my freewheeling style; the old guard detested everything about me.
As usual, I didn't try real hard to win anyone over.

Then in late spring a call came from my sister, who was living in
San Diego. My sixty-two-year-old father had been diagnosed with
malignant melanoma, and things looked bad back on Long Island.
My sister, a nurse, was pregnant with her first child, so there was
no way she could get back home for an extended stay. My mother
was lost.

I met with the station boss, Tom Dargan, to tell him I had to break
the contract and go back home. Really, what else could I do? There
was no question that, alone, my mother was not going to be able to
handle my father's last days.

When the announcement of my departure was made, I was
stunned by some of the vicious comments. Idiots in the *Oregonian*
newspaper printed anonymous quotes from a few KATU people
who claimed that I had been fired. In those accounts, my father's
illness was being portrayed as a ruse to cover the mistake of hir-
ing O'Reilly. Of course, nobody would say that with their name
attached, because they would definitely have been paid a visit by
me. And they knew it.

Rage does not even begin to describe how I felt. But there was
nothing I could do: you can't confront phantoms. So I worked out my
final weeks, swallowing the unfairness. It did not go down well.

A few weeks after I got back to New York, my father died at

KATU
Television Center

Thomas R. Dargan
Executive Vice President —
Broadcasting/Portland

July 3, 1985

Ms. Carole Cooper
N.S. Bienstock, Inc.
10 Columbus Circle
New York, New York 10019

Dear Carole:

For the record, I wish to note that we are releasing Bill O'Reilly from his commitment to us due to the grave illness of his father; we had hoped Bill could have been with us longer.

You should know that in my opinion (based on thirty-five years' experience) O'Reilly is the most talented on-the-air anchor with whom I have worked.

He is also intelligent, energetic, conscientious and dedicated to high standards of conduct, both personal and professional.

Sincerely,

Thomas R. Dargan

TRD/jlh

home. At the end, my mother, sister, and I were at his side. The funeral was three days later. The ordeal was brutal on my mom; in fact, she never fully recovered. I hung around home that summer, making sure chaos was kept to a minimum so that my mother could deal with her grief without distraction. I took care of the financial stuff and tried in other ways to make her transition as soft as possible.

Along the way, things began to happen. Good things. The brass at WCVB-TV in Boston, Jim Coppersmith and Phil Balboni, offered me a challenging job at Channel 5. Also, I had been accepted into Harvard's Kennedy School of Government across the Charles River in Cambridge. So I decided to take a few courses there and work at the same time. Boston is just two hundred miles from New York, so getting home on a regular basis wasn't a problem.

In addition, my agent, Carole Cooper, had received a letter from KATU. It went as follows:

> Dear Carole:
>
> For the record, I wish to note that we are releasing Bill O'Reilly from his commitment to us due to the grave illness of his father; we had hoped Bill could have been with us longer.
>
> You should know that in my opinion (based on thirty-five years' experience) O'Reilly is the most talented on-the-air anchor with whom I have worked.
>
> He is also intelligent, energetic, conscientious and dedicated to high standards of conduct, both personal and professional.
>
> Sincerely,
> Thomas R. Dargan

That letter humbled me and tempered every bitter thought I had over the unfairness in Portland. You see, sometimes life is like that. When they kick you, and there's nothing you can do about it, a white knight rides in. Tom Dargan passed away a few years ago, but his kindness will stay with me for the rest of my life.

Life is indeed unfair, and nothing is going to change that. But if we ourselves strive to be fair, things will balance out. I really believe that. It all goes back to Moses and Jesus, doesn't it? Love your neighbor as you love yourself. When people ask me what drives my fierce work ethic, why I work so hard when I don't have to anymore, I simply tell them that I'm still on a quest to make sure others get treated fairly.

In a world that increasingly celebrates selfishness and excessive materialism, I don't do that. I'm with the guys on the front lines in Iraq and Afghanistan. I'm with the nuns and priests attending to the poor in Haiti. I'm for the moms and dads working sixty hours a week trying to improve the lives of their children. While I have my forum in the media, those people will be celebrated and get a fair hearing every day.

In your life, when the bastards pound you, fight back. But fight back smart. Remember where you came from and figure out where you want to go. Along the way, help everyone you can help. If you do that, a knight like Tom Dargan will ride in when you really need one. I guarantee it.

END OF STORY

Say good night, Gracie.

—GEORGE BURNS

He's a work in progress." How many times have you heard someone spout that bad cliché? What a copout. What it really means is, "He's a jerk and might be one forever." So never say that about anyone. We are all flawed; no person on this earth will ever be a completed "work." Just had to get that off my chest.

Writing this book was difficult for me. As you may know, I don't like to get into a lot of personal stuff. When *People* magazine interviewed me a few years ago, I pretty much stonewalled on the nonwork stuff and wouldn't even let them photograph my daughter's face.

That's because, as Boz Scaggs sang, "puttin' your business in the street" is low-down. Personal stuff should stay personal. Splattering your life all over the place never works out well. In this book, I tried to stay focused on how my life experiences have shaped my thinking on issues and the pursuit of justice. I hope I've succeeded in that.

At the end of my books, I like to thank the reader. After all, it's a great compliment that you would invest your money, time, and energy reading my story. Truly, I hope some of my adventures clicked with you—I hope you can use some of what's in this book to make things better in your life. Every one of us is on the planet for a purpose. I was lucky enough to find mine fairly young in life, but understanding the full of extent of my purpose took much longer.

Early in my career, I wasn't focused on the big picture as I am today. That was natural, since I was trying to find my way through the TV jungle, and the foliage was dense. But always I reacted when I saw someone treated unfairly. It is that passion, more than anything else, that has made me successful. Folks can feel it through their television screens. You might not like me, but it's obvious there's a real person looking right back at you. Sometimes, though, he's cranky.

Things I Wish I'd Known Earlier

To wrap up this book, I want to dispense a few tips. . . .

Calling them "words of wisdom" would be a stretch, but you may find the following observations amusing. First of all, if you believe in God, you know that the Deity has set up life as a series of challenges for us. When we're young we have great energy, but we're usually stupid. That's what George Bernard Shaw meant when he said, "Youth is wasted on the young." Many of us wise up as we get older, but then naps become a priority. It's just the way it is and always has been.

In my fifth decade, I began having conversations with myself. I should have started sooner, but I was too busy talking *about* myself to figure out that conversing honestly *with* yourself is a very fine tool for self-evaluation. So if you see me mumbling while walking down the street, that's what that's all about. And these conversations are tough. Often, they're about what I *should* have done. Monday-morning quarterbacking. Hey, meathead, you should have asked Hillary Clinton *this*; how could you have forgotten to hammer President Bush with *that*?

Questioning yourself sharply keeps the mind sharp. It creates a personal no-spin zone. Make a mistake? Identify the reason you made it. Then it's less likely to happen again. Rationalizing is stupid. That's what children do. I can't tell you how many times folks call me on the radio trying to justify bad behavior by pointing to other bad behavior.

"O'Reilly, how can you blame Iran for killing American soldiers when we supported the shah in 1956?" That kind of nonsense.

Another thing I've learned rather late in life is to rehearse stuff. No, not my TV script, but real life. Say you're going on a date. Well, think about the person you'll be with: what are his or her interests? Consider the evening carefully before you begin socializing.

Same thing at work. If you have a big event there, think about how you're going to approach it. You don't have to memorize stuff; just walk your mind through the schedule. You'll be amazed at how much more relaxed you'll become, and as some of us know, a calm mind leads to creativity.

Sadly, I didn't do any of that as a younger person. I just *barged* in there. I still feel sorry for some of my dates. By the time I actually figured out who they were, it was closing time. Often, my self-absorption was truly amazing. Luckily, I was fairly entertaining in a shallow kind of way, so I got away with some foolish behavior. The standard line my friends have about me is, "Well, you know what he's *like*." Indeed.

But, really, it's so easy to look forward and learn from the past. Just talk to yourself once in a while. Level with you. I know that sounds like the title of a dopey self-help book, but it's a worthwhile strategy.

Remember that song "The Gambler"? The key lines are these:

> You got to know when to hold 'em, know when to fold 'em,
> know when to walk away, and know when to run.

Now, I'm not a big Kenny Rogers fan because I can't get past the plastic surgery, and the chicken was just so-so, but there's plenty of wisdom in that chorus from his 1978 hit song. Especially when it comes to dealing (bad pun alert) with people.

Throughout my life, I've known some very great women who have gotten involved with flawed men. The ladies all had one thing in common: they simply would not acknowledge the guy's weaknesses when most everyone around them saw them clearly. The women either rationalized the bad behavior by saying things like, "Well, that's just the way Bruno is," or they ignored it entirely. Both responses *always* lead to disaster.

Men are another matter. They often let their, well, primitive drives do their thinking, if you know what I mean . . . and I think you do (as Joe Bob Briggs put it). For both sexes, the ability to read people is a survival necessity in our complicated world; there's no question about it. But keep in mind a couple of things. Most folks do not change. Hitler was a bad person from the jump. Evil is not acquired. It is enthusiastically embraced by evildoers. For some reason, they enjoy harming people. The dope dealer selling meth or heroin to a kid (or even to an adult) is not misguided. He or she is evil.

When it came to social concerns or situations, it was rare for my father to offer advice. But he did tell me this: "Watch how a person treats his mother. If he can't treat her decently, you don't want to know him."

You can add this to that: Watch how adults treat children. If a man abandons his child, there is no coming back for him; he's swine. Same thing for a mother. And if an adult abuses a kid, nothing can turn that evil around, because damaging a child lasts forever.

I'm thankful I've always had good instincts when it comes to associating with others. As we've discussed, most of my friends are longtime amigos. Of course, I've made some mistakes in evaluating folks and have paid the price. But when it comes to friends, I've always had high standards, and that has saved me much heartache and betrayal. But know this: I'd rather be alone than be with someone I can't trust. I am comfortable solo.

So when someone you know does something wrong, beware. Don't just overlook it. Find out more. And if the conduct continues, quickly cut your losses, even if you are not the target of the bad stuff. Because, in the end, a deeply flawed person, one who embraces and excuses bad behavior, will get around to hurting you. The scorpion will sting, because it's his nature. Have no doubt.

When I was a young guy, I lived on fast food. Burgers, fries, deep-dish pizza, and fried seafood dominated my diet. Don't do that. Food affects everything you do and will kill you early if you don't wise up.

As a bachelor, I never cooked. Never even thought about it. Why cook if Burger King is over there? So I ate in restaurants all the time, chowing down on whatever tasted good. That meant loads of salt and sugar, not too many Brussels sprouts. Even when I visited Brussels, I avoided the sprouts. I ate fries.

With that diet, it is truly a miracle that I am still walking around. These days, I'm not exactly Jack LaLanne, juicing up all my meals, but most of the time I avoid fast food. And when I do succumb, my stomach punishes me for two days.

Of course, as a predictable baby boomer, I blame the bad diet of my younger days on my parents. As you may know, boomers are big on laying their bad habits off on Mom and Dad. In my house, we were big on the Mediterranean diet. Kind of. It was only after

I had actually traveled to Italy and Greece that I figured out ravioli doesn't always come in a can, and if you order SpaghettiOs in Naples, someone will hit you.

Anyway, my folks ate what their folks ate, which was inexpensive food blasted with salt. In the summer, barbecues were big. On Sunday, some kind of roasted meat made an appearance. If Rachael Ray lived in my house, she would have been in tears every day of her life.

Above all, there was a culinary routine. The following menu was fairly consistent in the O'Reilly house. Please keep in mind that my mother bought cereal in the economical "ten-packs."

Sunday
Breakfast: French toast, real maple syrup, bacon, and milk
Lunch: Campbell's chicken noodle soup, tuna sandwich, chips
Dinner: Pot roast, mashed potatoes, Jolly Green Giant peas, ice-cream sandwich

Monday
Breakfast: Sugar Pops cereal, English muffin, grape jelly
Lunch: Bologna sandwich on white with mustard, chips, cookies
Dinner: Sloppy joes (if you don't know, you don't *want* to know)

Tuesday
Breakfast: Sugar Frosted Flakes cereal, crumb cake, butter
Lunch: Tuna sandwich, chips, cookies
Dinner: Pork chops, noodles "Romanoff" (fake cheese on noodles), canned wax beans, Jell-O with whipped cream

Wednesday
Breakfast: Rice Krispies cereal with sugar, Entenmann's jelly doughnuts (excellent)

Lunch: Ham and American cheese on white with mustard, chips, cookies

Dinner: Hot dogs, baked beans, Tater Tots (awful), chocolate pudding

Thursday

Breakfast: Cocoa Puffs cereal, white toast with strawberry jam

Lunch: Olive loaf on white with mustard, chips, cookies

Dinner: Tuna "casserole," green beans or lima beans or string beans, ice pop

Friday

Breakfast: Cornflakes with sugar, frozen waffles with real maple syrup

Lunch: Tuna sandwich with lettuce, chips, cookies

Dinner: Fish sticks (breaded and dreaded), spaghetti with canned tomato sauce

Saturday

Breakfast: Scrambled eggs, sausage, white toast

Lunch: Hot dogs or hamburgers

Dinner: Flank steak, baked potato, beans of some kind, Entenmann's chocolate cake (extraordinary)

Also, there were a variety of Hostess and Drake's snacks available in my house, which were often used as bribes to "calm down" us kids. Big items were Ring Dings, Sno Balls, Devil Dogs, Twinkies, and Hostess CupCakes. Of course, the sugar rush provided by these waist busters did little to calm down any kid. In fact, they'd keep you up another couple of hours at night. Loved them.

If it's true that "you are what you eat," then I am one sweet guy, simply because of cereal intake alone. Today, however, I am big on healthful food. Oatmeal in the morning, soups with vegetables for lunch, and nonfried fish for dinner. I've always been a boring guy, and now I am even more so. I still love cheeseburgers, but if I eat one every five weeks, that's a lot. Tragically, there are no longer any Ring Dings in my house.

If I could, I'd eat nachos every day. But I can't. I work sixty hours a week, and my fuel has to be premium. Nutritious food is the most important factor in staying healthy. I wish I had known that at age twenty-five. But, again, it was my parents' fault that I did not.

Perhaps my antismoking, antidrinking posture slightly mitigated the junk-food diet. My mother smoked at least a pack a day, so my sister and I became well acquainted with secondhand smoke while sitting in the backseat of the family's Nash Rambler. Combined with the car's extensive exhaust fumes, the clouds of cigarette smoke made it seem like Shanghai back there. But remember, in the 1950s and 1960s, smoking was *expected.* If you weren't puffing away, folks in Levittown would wonder what *exactly* was wrong with you. Even my father would have a Marlboro once in a while, although he never became addicted, as my mother did.

As for drinking, there was lots of it among adults in the neighborhood, but my parents were always sober. My mother would have a little wine now and then; my father would drink Piels beer at dinner. However, my dad made it clear to us that anyone who got drunk was a lush. In my house, that was not a good thing.

Of course, most kids in Levittown sneaked cigarettes out of the house and would smoke them in the woods or wherever. I did that for a very short time but found it boring and truly distasteful. I never cared about being "cool," so wasting time puffing on a Winston had zero appeal for me. Therefore, after a few dopey trips to the forest, I banished cigarettes forever.

Throughout my teen years, it basically came down to orange soda, Carvel ice cream, and double cheeseburgers. The diet of champions. Since I played four sports, I didn't get fat. Since I played four sports,

I didn't get high. But, sad to say, there was nothing the sports could do about my personality.

The nuns were fond of saying that cleanliness was next to godliness, but few in my class cared much about that. But the nuns were cor-rect! Grooming is so important in America that I wish, as a kid, I had been subject to some formal training in it rather than just plati-tudes. We had one bathroom in my house, and to call it small is to insult Mickey Rooney.

Because my father was at heart a military man, daily showers were required, but looking spiffy was not a top priority. And since all my friends looked like me, who even knew what spiffy looked like? Of course, Ann-Margret was plenty spiffy, but, hey, that was Hollywood, not Long Island. Most of us in Levittown had pale white complexions topped with bad haircuts and that was that. Once Elvis appeared on the scene, the haircuts got even worse. And don't even mention the Beatles.

It was upon entering Chaminade High School in 1963 that I first saw the flip side of grooming. After phys ed, we were required to take showers. Presto, an astonishing array of grooming stuff ap-peared in the locker room, thanks to the rich guys. Sprays and gels and lotions were all set in motion. Up to that point in my life, I understood Johnson's baby powder, but that was about it. However, the swell guys had all kinds of exotic personal products, and even had nifty little compact leather cases in which to store them. Wow.

All men are created equal, but from then on, training makes the difference. Ask any Marine, Navy SEAL, or Army Ranger and they will confirm that. My parents were clean and neat, and my father might even slap on a little Aqua Velva or something in the morning. But, again, in my house there was little emphasis on appearance or personal presentation. And, again, this is very important in America. So working-class kids like me were behind the grooming curve. I believe this remains the case today all throughout the country.

Living in London during the 1969–70 college term drastically altered the bold, fresh guy's "presentation." British students typically dressed in Harris tweed jackets and flared trousers. At the time, prices were very low in Great Britain, so my American dorm mate, Edgar Royce, and I cruised Oxford Street for groovy clothes and actually bought some. This was a far cry from Mays department store in Levittown.

When I returned to Marist College for my senior year, my new wardrobe won me points with some of the coeds, who were used to seeing college boys dressed like gardeners. But you should have seen the looks from my guy friends when I showed up to my Marriage and the Family class wearing a blue blazer. Priceless.

The United States is a great country that honors values and freedom, but many Americans also worship attractive looks. So please understand that appearance and speech are ultra-important to achieving success. In my early youth, I spoke with a pronounced New Yawk accent and dressed like one of the Dead End Kids. My parents regarded that as a matter of course, simply the natural order of things. But the more quickly you figure out that you will be judged by how you look and how you sound, the easier your life will be. Santana might get away with singing, "ain't got nobody that I can depend on." But you can't. That is, if you want to work in the lucrative white-collar world.

These days when I go to the beach, I see many young kids covered with garish tattoos and showing off pierced faces. What are their parents thinking? Someday, one of those beach kids might want to earn some decent money by working for the *Factor.* Let me be blunt: a dragon tattoo on your neck is not gonna help in that quest. I remain a working-class guy by choice, but my staff has to present itself in a certain way, because we are dealing with some of the most powerful people on earth. Street smarts are great, but looking like you just got paroled from Sing Sing is not. Life is hard enough. Don't make it more difficult by cutting down your vocational opportunities because you want to look like Eminem. Okay?

Finally, I want to tell you about one thing I still haven't mastered: patience. Even though I am successful and supposedly bright, I still let myself get annoyed in certain situations that I should simply disregard. For me, it's all about expectations. If I go to a restaurant, for example, and the service is bad, it ticks me off. I know, I know . . . I should just let it go, either leave or tough it out. But no, the bold, fresh guy often has to confront the manager and explain the source of my disenchantment. Usually, I do this quietly, but I still do it. Why? Because it is *not the way things should be.*

Now, I know this is stupid. So what if the steak tartare takes an hour to get out of the kitchen? Actually, I never eat anything tartare. That sounds like a band of ancient Asian marauders. But my point is that bad service is small stuff. And, as we all know, you don't sweat the small stuff.

But sometimes I do.

Jesus would not sweat the small stuff. Neither would Gandhi. They were big-stuff guys. Mostly, I try to be a big-stuff guy, too. But sometimes I fail.

Tardiness also drives me crazy. I should overlook it, but, somehow, I see it as an insult. Your time is more valuable than mine? I have to wait for you? Of course, things happen, and I am fine with valid reasons for delay. However, to be late just because you *can* eliminates you from my dance card.

When I interviewed Senator Hillary Clinton in late April 2008, she was forty-five minutes late. Her Secret Service guys told me she is almost always tardy. Of course, I was being well paid to wait for the senator, but I noted the situation. By the way, when Hillary finally showed up, she didn't mention being late. Interesting.

My father tended to sweat the small stuff, so, like the bad-food deal, maybe I can blame him; perhaps it's genetic. The nuns certainly sweated every little thing. Therefore, I feel comfortable blaming the Catholic Church for my impatience, which I believe is considered a venial sin. Remember, I am a baby boomer and, as noted earlier, we are the absolute best at assigning blame to others for our own failings. In fact, we have honed this technique to a degree never before seen in America.

If there's any good in being impatient, it's that it can help at work. The *Factor* staff is quick. No fooling around. When they get an assignment, boom, they're on top of it. Partly, that's because they don't want me prodding them with salty language, but mostly it's about pride. We do three hours of commentary a day—one on television, two on radio—and always meet our deadlines. In my opinion, the *Factor* staff is the gold standard in the TV news industry. Our ratings prove it.

For the most part, though, patience is a good thing. Patient people are often kind and accepting of the faults of others. They are soothing people. They like wind chimes and hot tea. Sometimes, they live in places like Big Sur, California, where they can look out at the sea and see stuff. They can do this for a long time, as there is no rush. Patience, as somebody once said, is its own reward.

But I am not patient, and it is primarily my father's fault.

I could go on with my story, but, as I like to say on the air, enough is enough. You've got it. A bold, fresh piece of humanity fights his way up and becomes a media force. Along the way, he has many adventures and encounters that have shaped his vision and philosophy.

If there is a CliffNotes for this book, I've just summed it up in this paragraph.

Again, thanks for taking the time to consider my story. I hope it was a good read. If it wasn't, tell someone you don't like that it was so they'll buy the book. Little things like that can bring satisfaction.

People always ask me what I do in my spare time. Well, I read, I collect American historical documents, I play some sports, I putter

around. Chances are I like the same stuff you like: sports, the beach, naps, and no spin.

For me there's no foie gras, no blinis, no four-dollar cups of coffee. And if there is any "fusion" involved in my supper, I will leave the table.

Of course, in my industry, there are plenty of swells who can't get enough "fusion," and there's no shortage of pretentious entitlement. As you know by now, the bold, fresh guy does not go for that. On weekends, I eat at my local diners and delicatessens. I talk to guys like the Bear and John Blasi, both of whom I've known since we were five years old. I go to church and pray for patience.

Also, I say prayers of thanks for the miracle of the life I have lived. Not kidding about that. Next time you meet an atheist, tell him or her that you know a bold, fresh guy, a barbarian who was raised in a working-class home and retains the lessons he learned there. Then mention to that atheist that this guy is now watched and listened to, on a daily basis, by millions of people all over the world and, to boot, sells millions of books.

Then, while the nonbeliever is digesting all that, ask him or her if they *still* don't believe there's a God!

Sister Lurana would be proud of that challenge to the atheist; I absolutely know that. So, if you really examine it, things have come full circle. The bold, fresh guy is still that way, but now, in front of millions, he's spouting life lessons born of his teachers and his parents.

There's something downright poetic about that. Is there not?

POSTSCRIPT

The usual suspects helped greatly in assembling this book, and I will mention them in a moment. But first I have to thank my ancestors. Really. Without them you might be reading a book by Dr. Phil instead of this one. So you should honor my ancestors as well.

My great-grandfather, John O'Reilly, was born in County Cavan, Ireland, in 1870. He emigrated (legally) to the USA and became a saloon keeper, marrying Isabelle Sullivan in 1892. They lived in Brooklyn.

My grandfather, John Jr., was born the following year, 1893. He subsequently had five siblings. At age twenty-seven, John O'Reilly Jr. married Gertrude McLaughlin, and they settled on West Street in Brooklyn. As mentioned, my grandfather was a New York City cop who patrolled the harbor.

My father, William J. O'Reilly, was born in 1924, the middle child in the family. He married my mother, Winifred Angela Drake, in 1947 at St. Patrick's Cathedral, a couple of blocks from where I work these days.

On my mother's side, things are murkier. Her ancestors, the Kennedy clan, began leaving Ireland during the great famine of the 1850s, subsequently settling in upstate New York and northeastern

Pennsylvania. The small town of Wappingers Falls, New York, became a haven for many of my mother's people.

As I stated, all of my ancestors were working-class folks. I am the first one to break out of that group, at least on paper.

Now, assembling all the stuff in this book wasn't easy, and I counted on my wife, Maureen, my assistant Makeda Wubneh, and the best editor in the country, Charles Flowers, to get me through it. Also, my agent, Eric Simonoff, and Broadway Books guy Gerry Howard helped immensely.

So, all of the above are partially responsible for this book, and you should blame them if you didn't like it. Don't blame me, because other people forced me to be the way I am. Shifting blame is the time-honored boomer way, and I am taking that con to the grave. Count on it: my death will be somebody else's fault. Wait and see.

Finally, you should know that I have set up a charitable foundation named for my parents. Each year we give hundreds of thousands of dollars to charities that help children, veterans, the poor, and the troubled. We also help noble agencies like Doctors Without Borders and Habitat for Humanity.

I am proud to do this, and I hope my father's spirit knows about it. Because he would be proud too.

Bill O'Reilly
Summer 2008

© Lynn Youngen

BILL O'REILLY, a three-time Emmy Award winner for excellence in reporting, served as national correspondent for ABC News and as anchor of the nationally syndicated news magazine program *Inside Edition* before becoming executive producer and anchor of Fox News's breakout hit *The O'Reilly Factor.* He is the author of the mega-bestsellers *The O'Reilly Factor, The No Spin Zone, Who's Looking Out for You?,* and *Culture Warrior,* as well as *Kids Are Americans Too, The O'Reilly Factor for Kids,* and the novel *Those Who Trespass.* He holds master's degrees from Harvard's Kennedy School of Government and Boston University.